INSIDE NEW ZEALAND WILDLIFE

Many thanks to Marianna Terezow at GNS Science, Steve Trewick at Massey University, and of course my wife Barbara, for all the helpful comments and advice.

Published in 2021 by David Bateman Ltd
Unit 2/5 Workspace Drive, Hobsonville, Auckland 0618, New Zealand
www.batemanbooks.co.nz

ISBN 978-1-98-853886-0

Illustrations by Dave Gunson
Cover illustration: Takahē
Title page illustration: Kea skull
Cover designed by Dave Gunson and Alice Bell
Internal design by Alice Bell
Printed in China by Toppan Leefung Printing Ltd

INSIDE NEW ZEALAND WILDLIFE

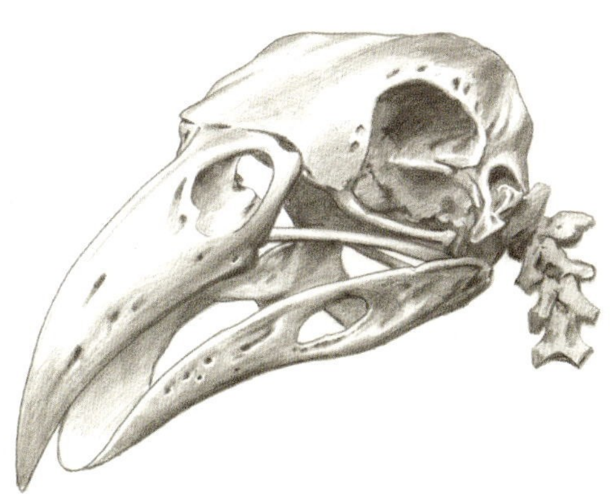

DAVE GUNSON

CONTENTS

INTRODUCTION

Among the multitude of wildlife species found in and around New Zealand, there's a great number that New Zealanders can easily recognise. Many — like the kiwi — are national icons, and they are celebrated as being simply 'ours'.

We know what they look like, what they do, where they live, and so on.

But do we really know how they 'work'? Are those smaller creatures simple or complex . . . does an ordinary earthworm have a brain, for example? Why do spiders need so many eyes? Larger animals can be just as mysterious . . . how does a dolphin's echolocation actually work?

To find out what goes on 'in there', this book takes a look at the insides of just a few of the better-known representatives from a handful of different types — from the humble mushroom in our gardens, through plants, molluscs, crustaceans, insects, fish and birds, and on up to the mammals that live in our seas. Without conforming to a strict scientific progression, the chosen subjects generally go from the simplest to the more complex forms.

About the illustrations

The book covers a selection of different views and sections — in most cases, layers of muscles, fat and general body tissues have been removed, so that the internal workings and the simplified arrangements of structures or organs can be seen more clearly and show how the animal is 'built'.

So . . . why not take a look *inside?*

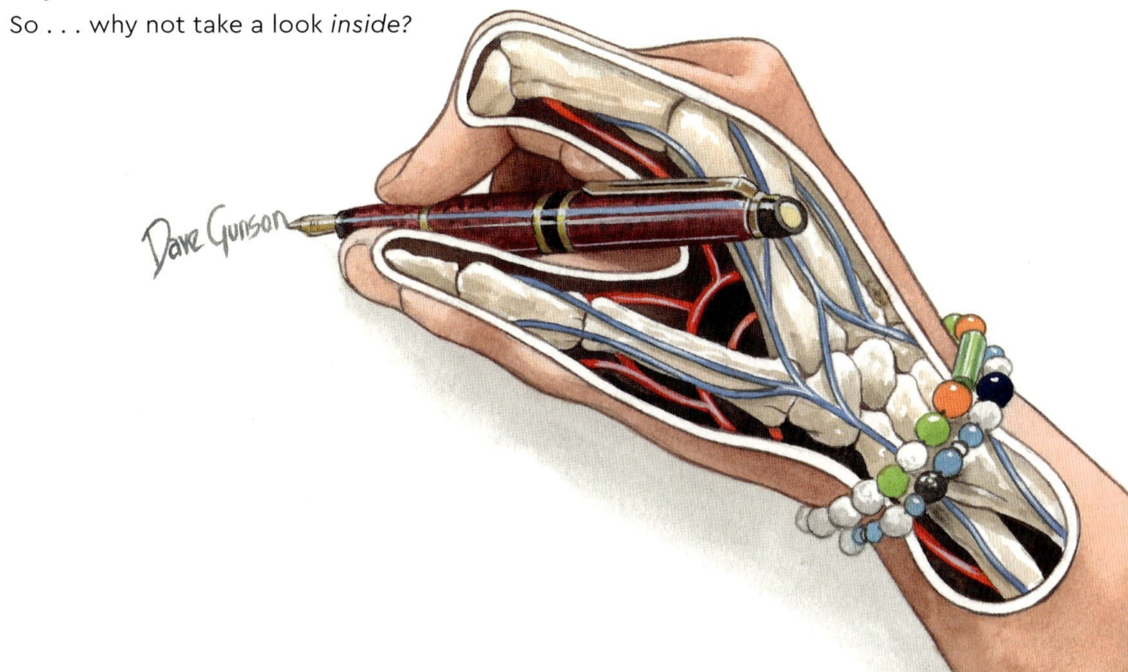

Fungal growths can appear in many sizes and shapes. Besides the typical mushroom shape, they can resemble open baskets, corals and rounded shelves on the sides of trees. They can be smaller than a speck of dust or almost too large and heavy to lift. There are about 20,000 fungi species in New Zealand, and about 300,000 known around the world.

Mushroom | harore

Mushrooms that you often see in gardens and parks are not plants, but fungi. They don't use sunlight and water for growth, as plants do, but instead they produce chemicals that can break down living or dead organic material to use as food.

The mushroom starts as a sort of bud, enclosed within a covering called a universal veil. As it gets bigger, the stem pushes up and breaks the veil, which will then form the mushroom's cap. Sometimes the stem keeps a ring of pieces of the veil — called an annulus. Rough scales or lumps sometimes seen on the mushroom's cap are also the remains of the veil. What's left of the veil at the base is called a cup, or volva.

When the mushroom is fully grown, the gills under the cap produce many millions of tiny spores. When they are released, they are carried about by the wind and eventually fall to the ground. Each spore then produces a tiny thread called a hypha. When hyphae from two spores connect, the thread-like mycelium is produced, and a new mushroom will then begin to develop.

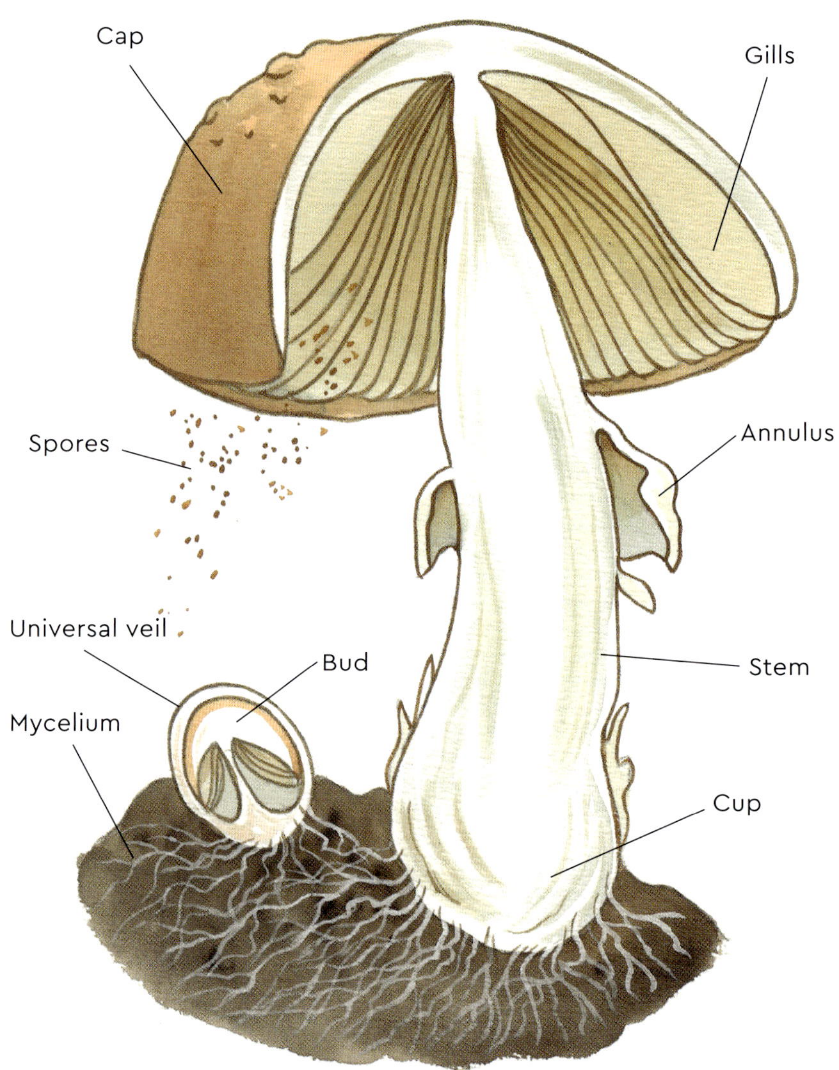

Mushrooms with very bumpy caps are often called toadstools. This is simply because those bumpy caps resemble the knobbly backs of some types of toad — they're not really stools for toads to sit on (but they could if they wanted to, of course).

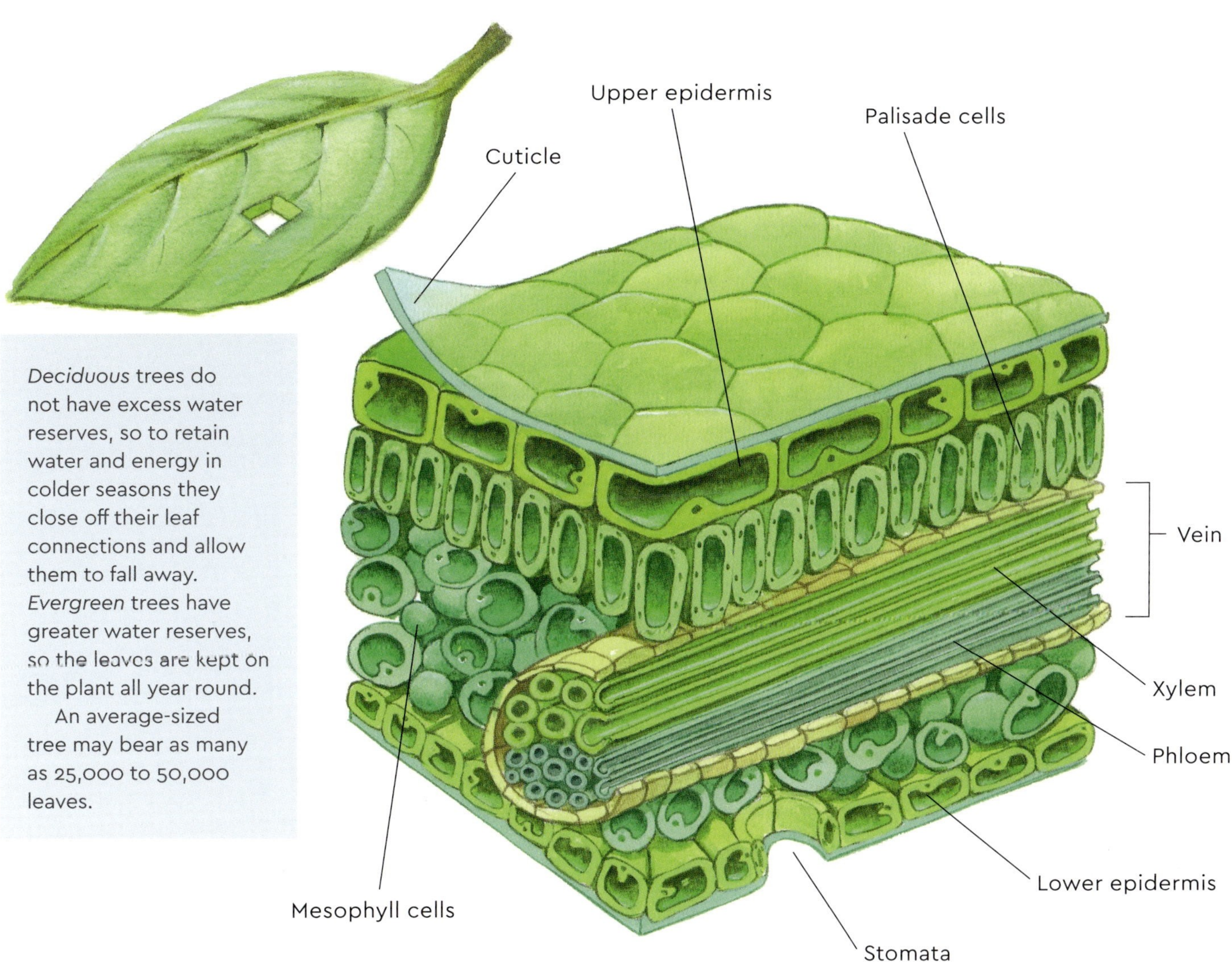

Deciduous trees do not have excess water reserves, so to retain water and energy in colder seasons they close off their leaf connections and allow them to fall away. *Evergreen* trees have greater water reserves, so the leaves are kept on the plant all year round.

An average-sized tree may bear as many as 25,000 to 50,000 leaves.

Leaves | rau

Leaves are the most important part of any plant. They provide the food supply that keeps a plant healthy and enables growth.

The leaves provide food through a process called photosynthesis. Chlorophyll — the substance that gives leaves their green colour — uses light energy to produce a chemical process which results in the necessary 'sugars' for the plant. Most of this process is carried out by the ranks of palisade cells, with the loosely arranged mesophyll cells 'assisting' in part of the process. The sugars are then carried throughout the plant by means of the phloem, while water and nutrients are drawn up from the plant's underground roots through the xylem. Together, the phloem and xylem form the veins that you can see on nearly any leaf.

The upper and lower epidermis (skin) of the leaf is protected by a fine, clear layer called a cuticle. The leaves have thousands of tiny holes (stomata) in their undersurfaces, which release oxygen into the atmosphere, and draw in carbon dioxide (the gas that we humans breathe out) as part of the process of photosynthesis.

Trees | rākau

Most trees follow a similar pattern of growth. Seeds dropped to the ground develop into simple growing plants, which develop roots to gain nutrients from the soil, and then produces leaves. Eventually a sapling — a young tree — appears and grows to become a mature tree.

Cut through the trunk of a tree and its history is shown. Each 'ring' represents a year of the tree's growth. When the rings are close together, this reveals years of poor growth — perhaps due to weather conditions or overcrowding from other trees. Rings further apart show periods of better growth.

The outermost dark ring of the tree trunk is called the cambium, which grows outward a little each year: its outer side (the bark) is hard and tough to protect the tree, while it produces new growth on the inside.

The innermost layer of the cambium is the phloem, which transports sugar sap from the leaves downwards through the tree to the roots, or through the branches to the developing flowers, and the layer next to the cambium is the xylem, which carries water upward. At the very centre is the pith — the softest new wood.

The rays that spread out from the trunk's centre transport and retain food for the tree.

The 'knots' and dents visible in cut wood are the scars from branches which have fallen, or they may be the result of damage from fires or lightning.

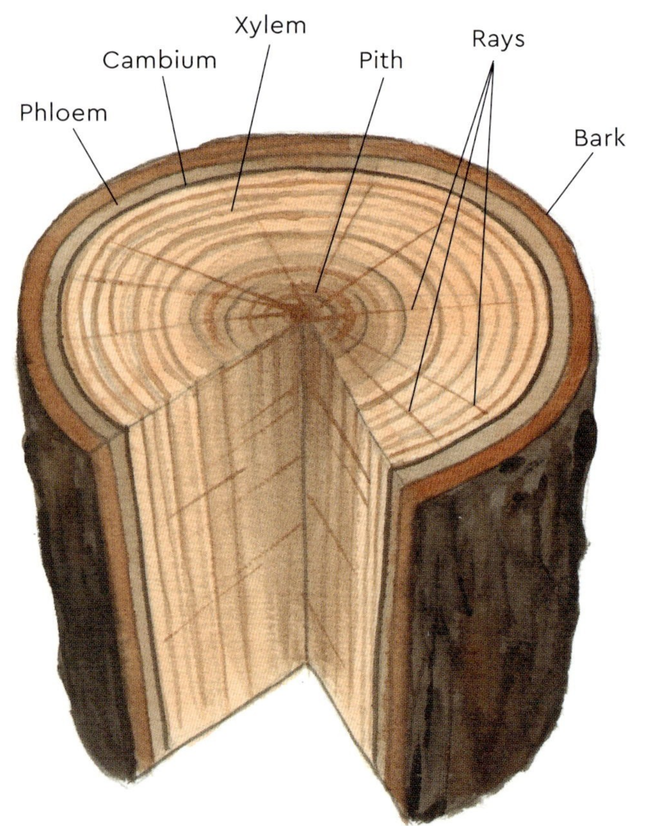

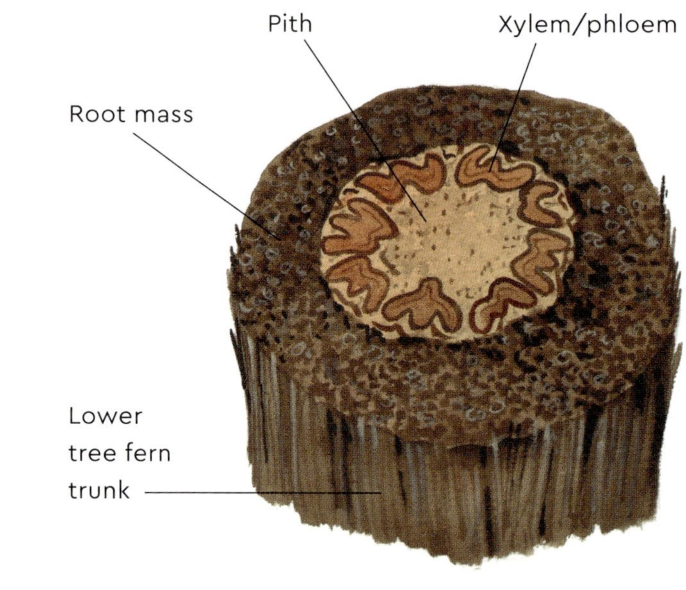

Tree ferns show a much simpler structure when cut. They reproduce from spores, not seeds, and have large fronds instead of complex leaves. The trunks usually consist of a thin, simple stem of spongy, 'woody' pith at its centre, with a xylem/phloem structure. The lower trunk is enclosed in thick roots, which continue to grow and expand as the tree fern rises. Further up, beyond the enclosing roots, the outer trunk bears the evidence or remains of fallen or discarded fronds.

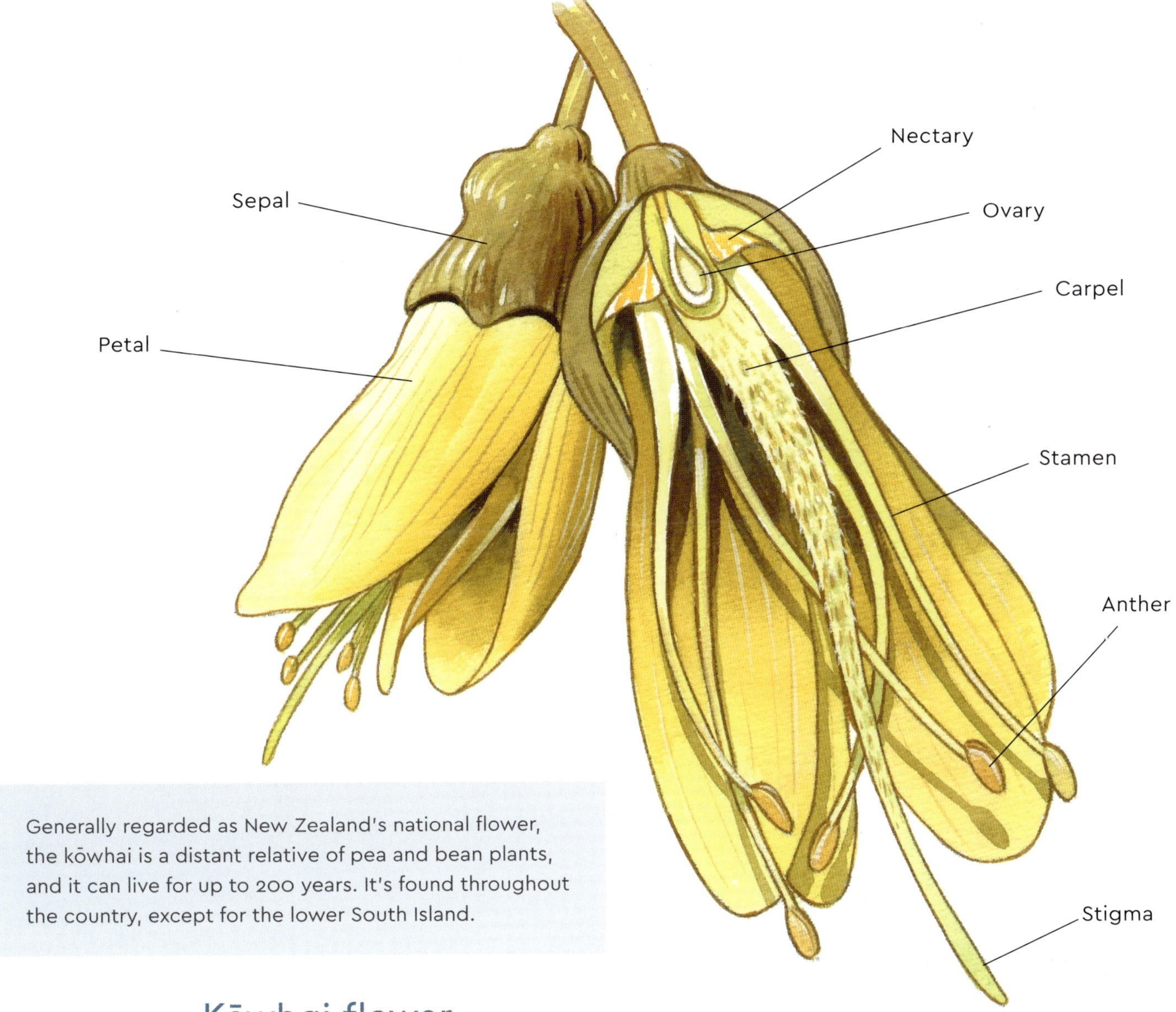

Generally regarded as New Zealand's national flower, the kōwhai is a distant relative of pea and bean plants, and it can live for up to 200 years. It's found throughout the country, except for the lower South Island.

Kōwhai flower

Many plants produce flowers as part of the process of reproduction — to produce new, young plants that are slightly different from the parent plant, which ensures that the species can survive and thrive in a range of changing conditions.

The flowers carry pollen, which needs to be combined with the pollen from another plant of the same type, for new fruit and seeds to develop. Some can be carried by wind, but many flowers have sweet nectar or pollen to attract birds or insects to visit, and these visitors transfer the pollen as they move from plant to plant.

The kōwhai tree produces nectar at the base of the flowers, to attract birds such as the tūī. The tūī has a long brush-tipped tongue to take up the nectar, and as it pushes its bill deep into the flower petals to take a sip, its head gets dusted with pollen grains from the anthers at the ends of the flower's many stamens.

When the bird then visits another flower, the pollen left on its head is caught by the stigma at the very end of a structure called a carpel. Now with a suitable mix of pollen, the ovary at the base of the carpel can develop the seeds needed for new kōwhai plants.

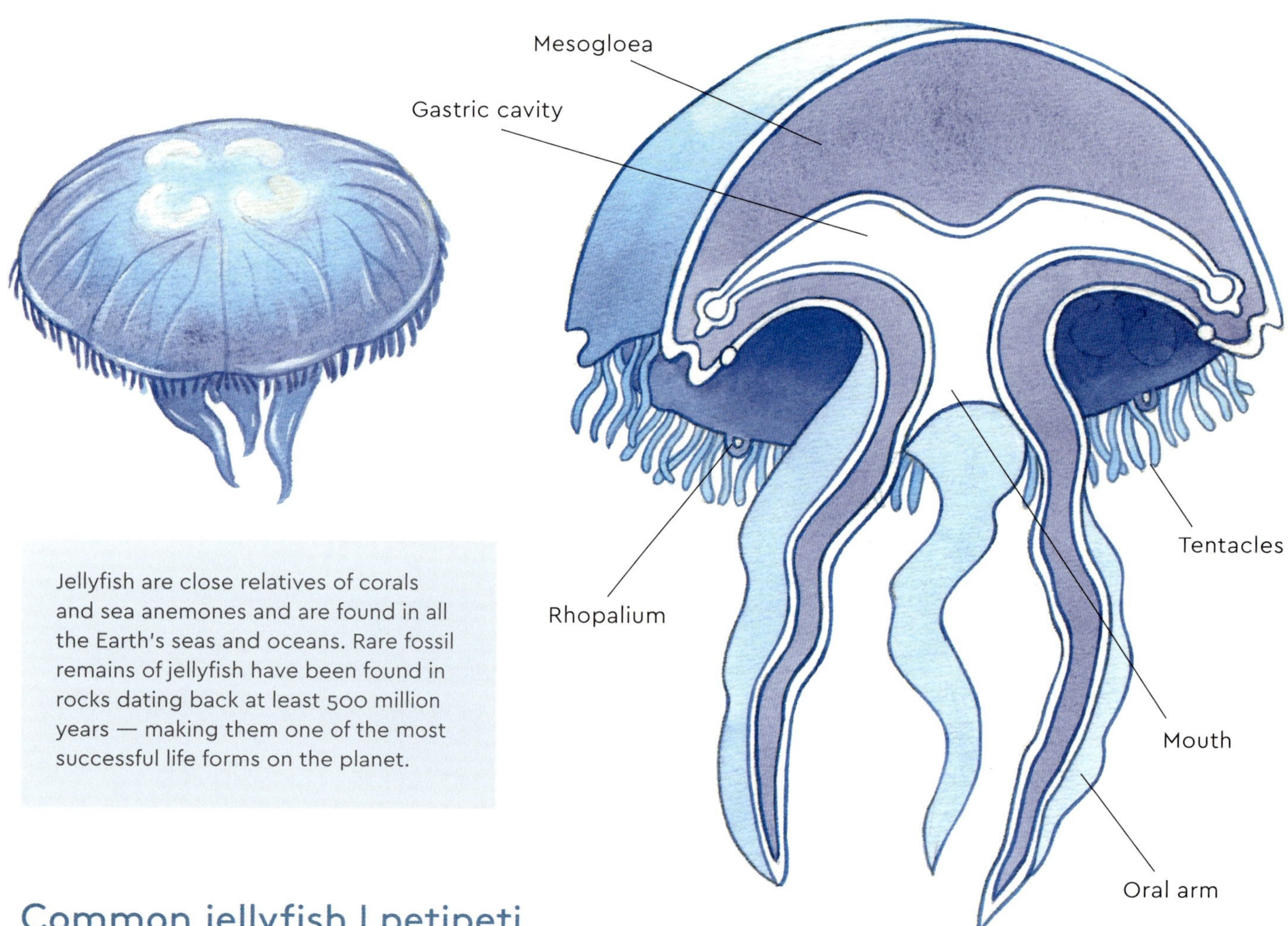

Jellyfish are close relatives of corals and sea anemones and are found in all the Earth's seas and oceans. Rare fossil remains of jellyfish have been found in rocks dating back at least 500 million years — making them one of the most successful life forms on the planet.

Common jellyfish | petipeti

Almost true to its name, the 20 centimetre-wide common jellyfish's distinctive shape in the water is maintained by a watery, jelly-like substance called the mesogloea, which contains muscle and nerve fibres.

The jellyfish has no heart, brains or blood, and its body consists of about 95 per cent water. A simple nervous system controls its movements and reactions.

It swims by contracting and relaxing a ring of muscles set around the bell-shaped body — water is drawn in and pushed out to provide motion. The rate of the contractions is set by the rhopalium, which can also sense light, vibrations and scents in the water. Some species of jellyfish may have up to 24 primitive rhopalium 'eyes' and can even distinguish shapes and colours.

The tentacles around the rim have stinging cells to stun and catch passing prey — such as small fish and tiny plant material — as do the long oral arms. The catch is then drawn up to the mouth opening and into the gastric cavity, where it is digested, and the nutrients are then transported around the body. Any waste is released back into the water through the mouth, which also functions as the animal's anus.

The gonads are seen as lighter ring shapes when the jellyfish is viewed from above, and they form part of the reproductive system.

Red beadlet sea anemone | kōtoretore

One of our most common sea anemones, the red beadlet can be found in rock pools around most of the country, often half-hidden under the overhangs around the edges. Belonging to the same animal grouping as corals and jellyfish, the sea anemone has stinging cells called nematocysts in its tentacles, which are arranged around an oral disc, supported by a body collar. It uses these tentacles to stun and capture tiny water creatures that come by.

The captured prey is then drawn into the mouth and down to the gastro-vascular cavity, where it is digested.

The anemone also has stinging cells in threads called acontia in its basal disc, which can be discharged through the mouth or body to ward off predators.

All around the body are retractor muscles, which can withdraw the tentacles inwardly, so that when the tide is out, the anemone simply appears as a blob of red jelly attached to the rock. It can safely remain this way until the tide returns.

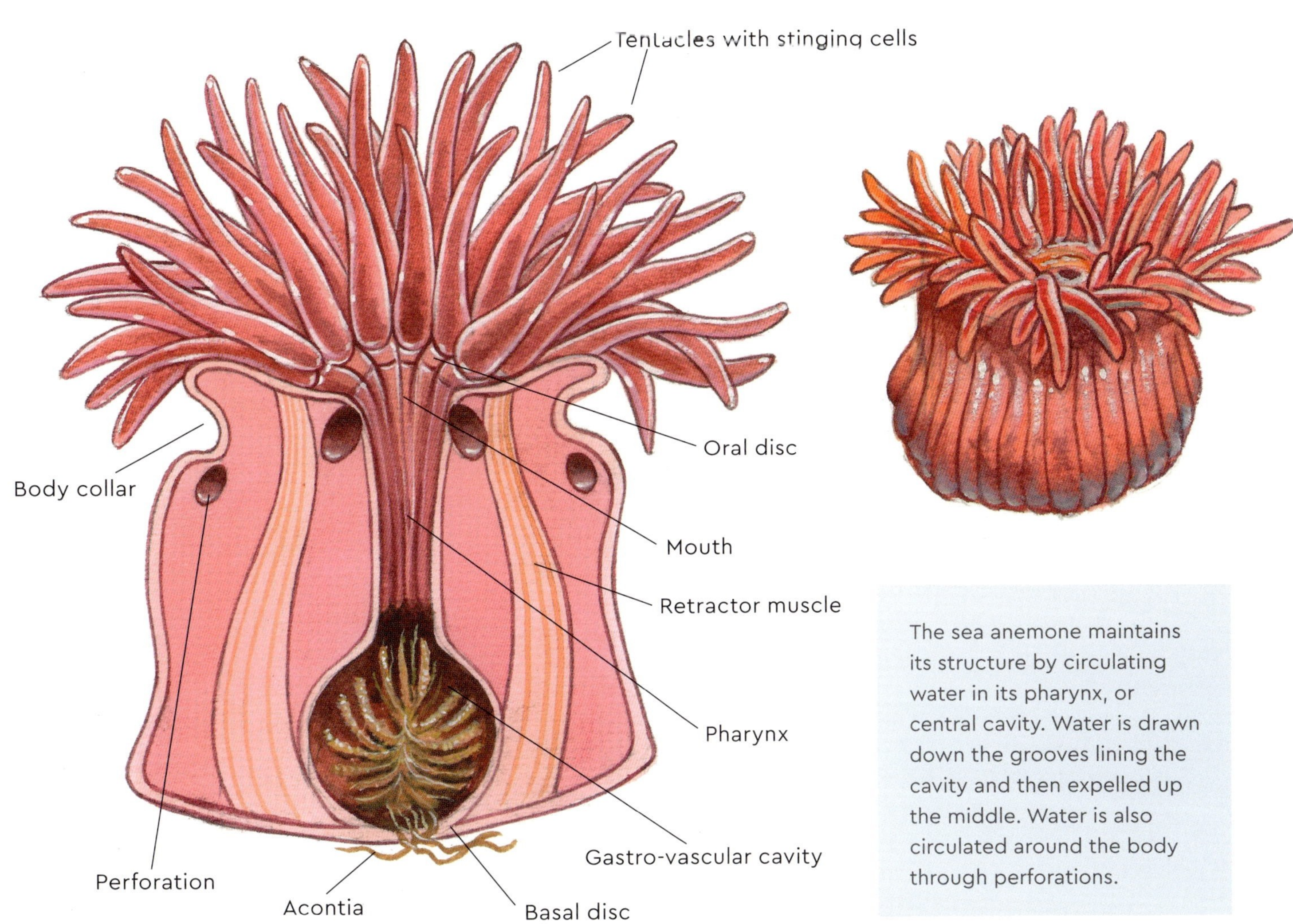

The sea anemone maintains its structure by circulating water in its pharynx, or central cavity. Water is drawn down the grooves lining the cavity and then expelled up the middle. Water is also circulated around the body through perforations.

Sea star | pātangaroa

A typical sea star (previously called starfish) has a five-part body symmetry, but many have more than just five arms — some species may have 7, 10, 20 and others may even have up to 40 arms.

Some sea stars can be seen with small stubs, where arms that have been lost due to accident or attack from predators are growing back. Some sea stars can even regenerate their body from just a portion of the central disc and a single surviving arm — although this regrowth can take up to a year.

The outer skin is usually tough and sometimes covered in spines to help protect the sea star from predators such as snapper and other fish, large shellfish, crabs, birds and even other, bigger, sea stars.

They use hundreds or thousands of tiny tube feet to move about the seabed, where they feed on kina, shellfish and other small animals and plant growths. A sea star can use its arms to prise open the two valves of a shellfish (see common cockle, page 18) to get at the animal inside. It will then push part of its stomach out of its mouth (located in the middle, underneath) to eat its prey, and then 'swallows' its stomach back inside to digest the food at leisure.

Inside each arm, the central and radial canals hold the ampulla, which control the many tube feet. Above these are the gonads (reproductive organs), and above these are the digestive glands.

The madreporite or sieve plate controls the amount of seawater in the body, which helps to regulate the pressure inside the body, and which is also pumped into the tube feet. The seawater also acts as a form of blood and carries nutrients throughout the rest of the body.

Although sea stars don't 'see' as we do, they have a simple reddish 'eye-spot' at the end of each arm, which can detect light and dark. But although they can't really see their prey, they have a very good sense of smell — special cells in their skin can detect even the faintest scent from any nearby shellfish, and then they take off in a crawling slow-motion attack towards their prey.

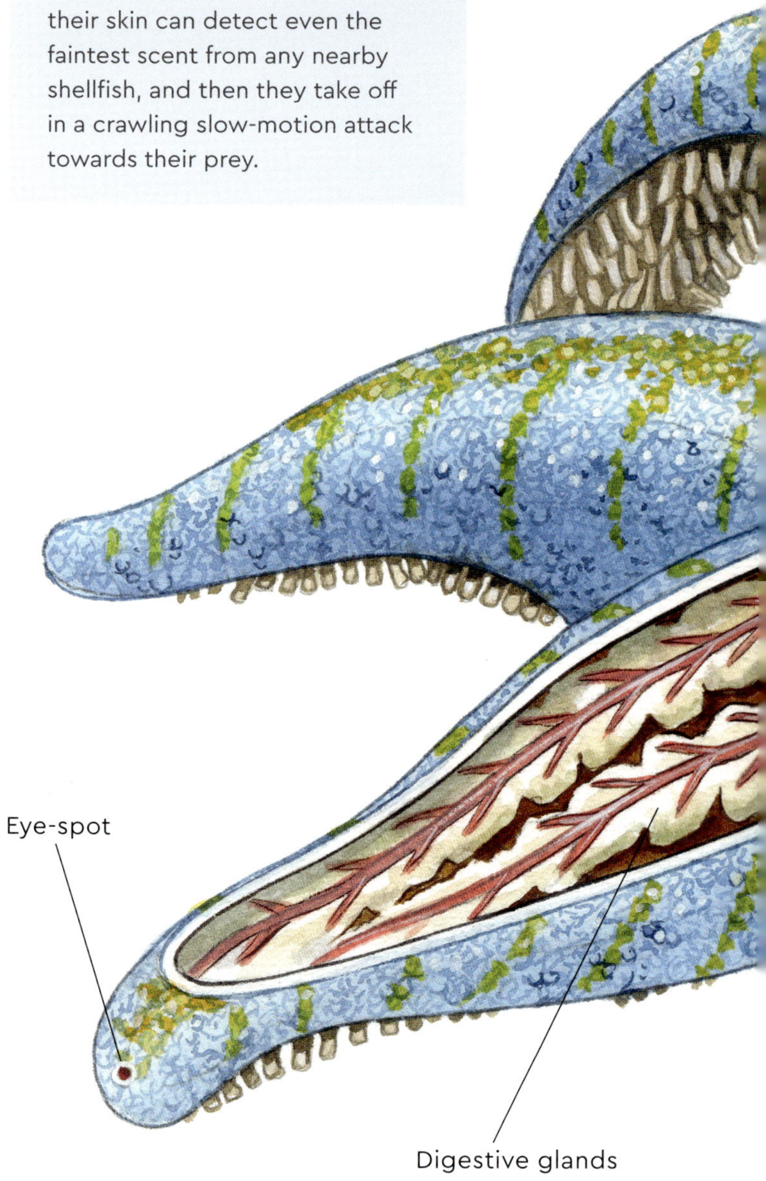

Eye-spot

Digestive glands

New Zealand has over 180 types of sea star, and around the world 2000 types of seas stars can be found in rock pools and shallow water, and even all the way down to depths of 6000 metres. They can live for anything between 10 and 35 years.

They have been found in fossil records dating back some 450 million years.

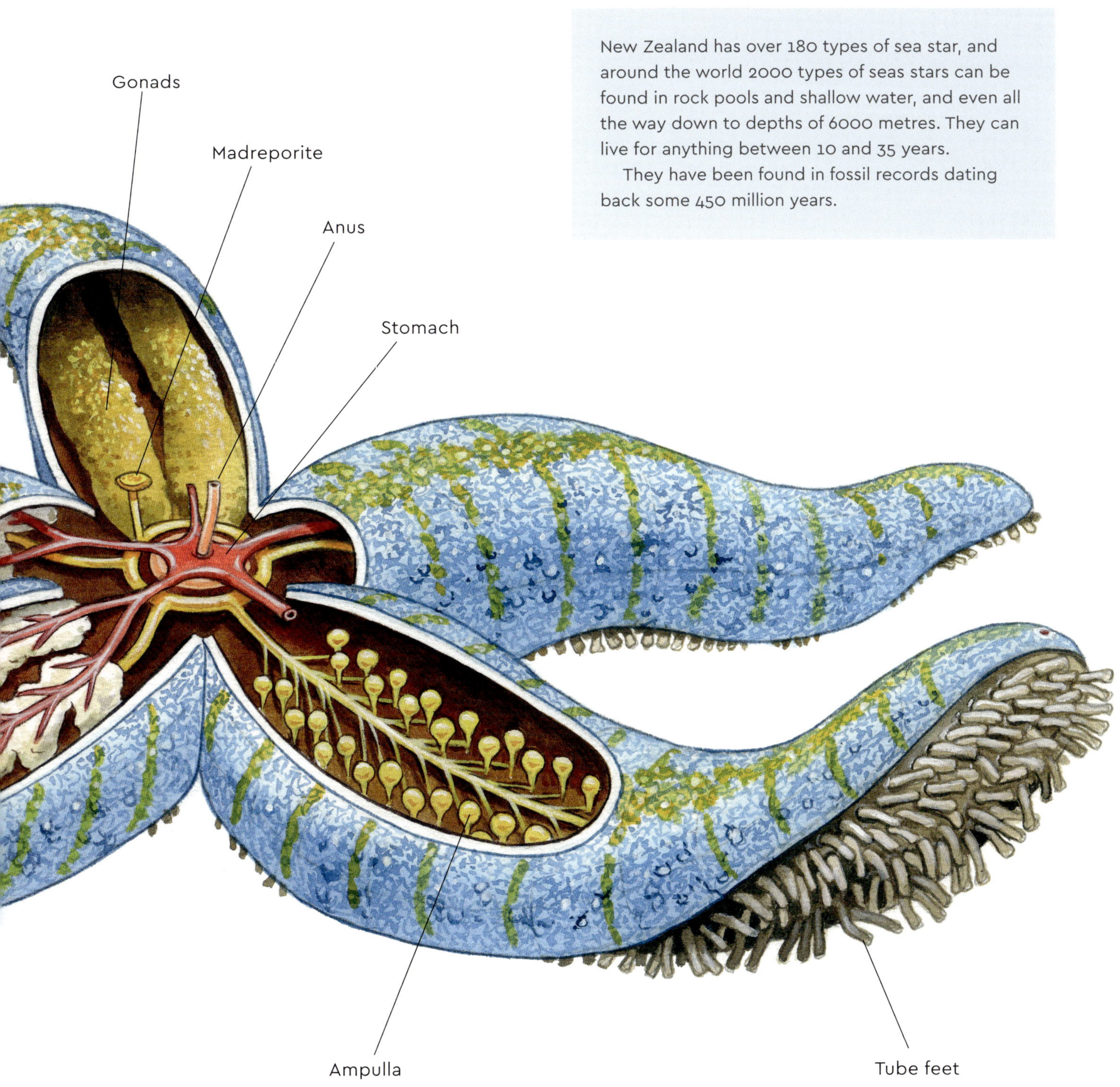

Common sea urchin | kina

New Zealand's common sea urchin — kina — can be found all around the coast in shallow waters and down to about 15 metres.

Kina feed mostly on seaweeds and will even climb kelp stems to reach the young fronds. Sometimes large populations — up to 50 kina per square metre at times — can devastate kelp forests and leave only bare rock remaining.

The hard outer body shell, called a test, is equipped with plenty of tough spines for protection. However, many predators — especially large sea stars, crayfish and snapper (and humans) — hunt kina for the tasty and brightly coloured roe (gonads) to be found inside. The roe is part of the kina's reproductive system. Whole and broken parts of the animal's test are commonly found on shores around the country.

Kina travel about by means of a multitude of tube-like feet that can be extended beyond the spines, which can also be moved to assist. The ring canal supplies water to the tube feet, and the nerve ring senses and directs movement.

Like the sea star (previous page), the kina has a five-part body symmetry, and a solid structure called Aristotle's lantern has five 'teeth' at its base for grazing and feeding.

Kina grow to about 10 to 15 centimetres across, and some may live for up to 20 years.

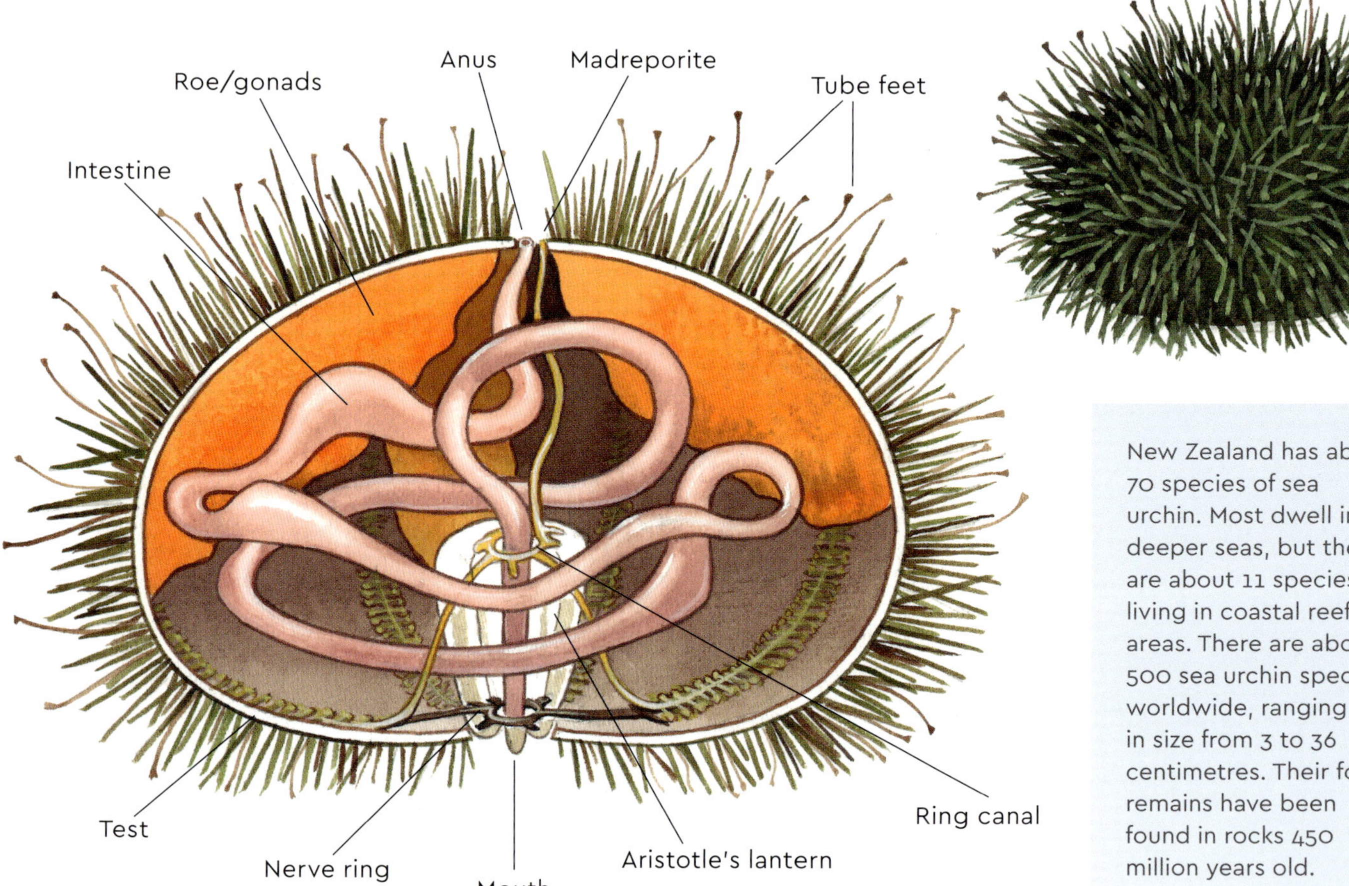

New Zealand has about 70 species of sea urchin. Most dwell in deeper seas, but there are about 11 species living in coastal reef areas. There are about 500 sea urchin species worldwide, ranging in size from 3 to 36 centimetres. Their fossil remains have been found in rocks 450 million years old.

Earthworm | noke

Matching its appearance, the common earthworm has a relatively uncomplicated and straightforward interior. It has a simplified five-part heart, and a basic digestive system — running straight from its mouth, crop (where food can be stored before digestion) and intestine, to its anus.

Worm faeces (poos) are deposited on the surface of the ground and are known as castings. Because the worm eats all sorts of organic material such as plant debris, the castings are rich in concentrated nutrients, and they can improve and enrich the soil. Worms can also release waste fluids through pores in the sides of their bodies.

Longitudinal muscles run the length of the body, so that the worm can thrust and withdraw as it pushes its way through the earth. Each body segment has a dividing partition (the septum) and a circular muscle, which allows it to expand and shrink its body width as it moves forward. Each body segment has two pairs of fine hairs — called setae — which assist in movement.

Lacking eyes, worms cannot see where they are going, but they are sensitive to light and dark.

Each earthworm is both male and female, but it needs to mate with another individual, and both will then produce eggs. The developing eggs are stored within a protective cocoon inside the saddle-like body ring (the clitellum) until they are ready to be laid.

Common garden earthworms can live for 2 to 8 years and measure between 20 and 350 millimetres in length. There are about 200 species of earthworm in New Zealand, and the largest is the seldom seen giant Northland worm, which can grow to 1.5 metres in length.

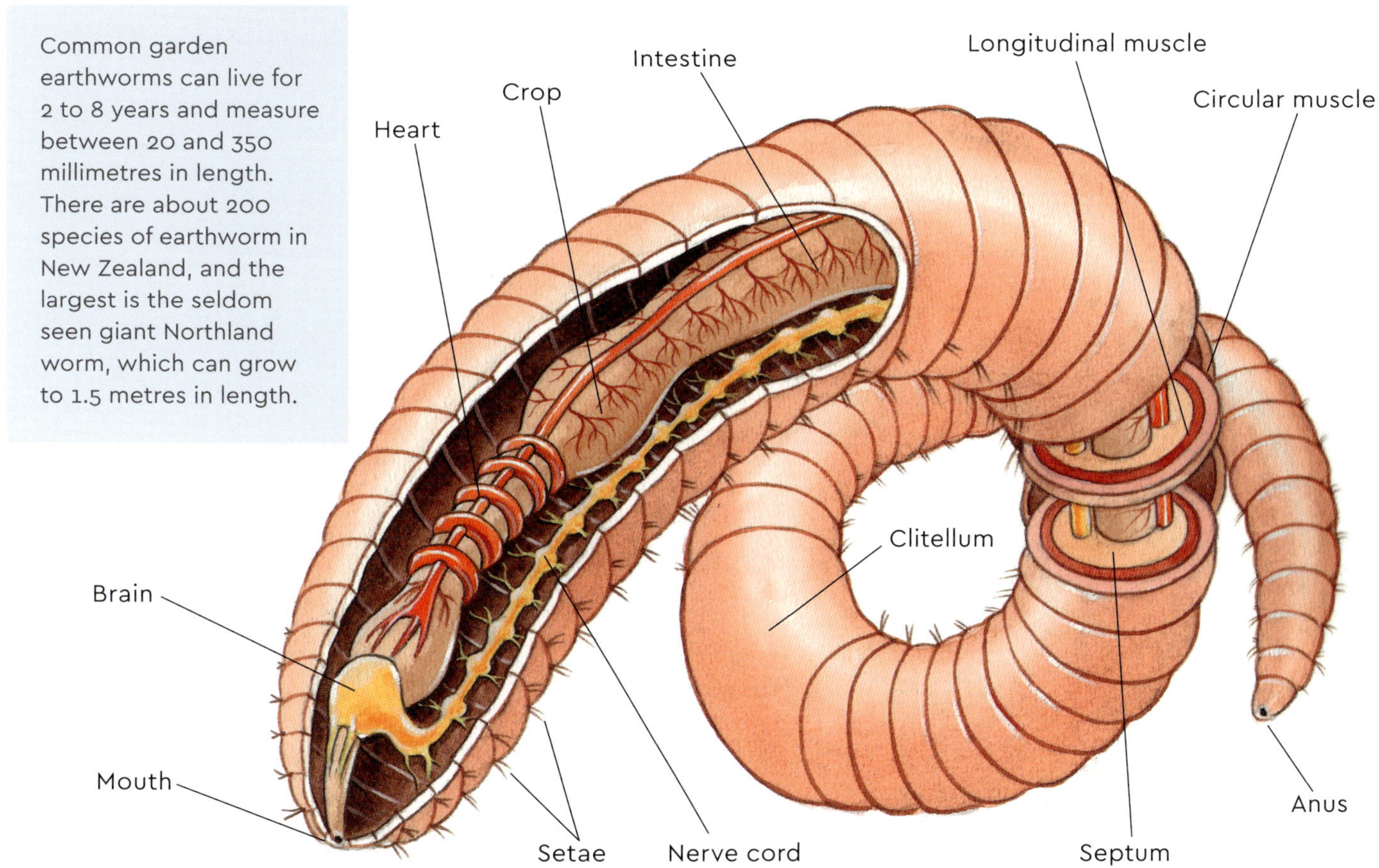

Garden snail | ngata kāri

Snails are members of an animal grouping — gastropods — that includes all the different types of shellfish. Snails are called univalves, as they have only one shell, or valve. Although New Zealand has about 1400 species of snails, the one most commonly seen is the garden snail — introduced here by early settlers from Europe.

The snail can slide about on its single muscular 'foot' with the help of a special mucus released from the pedal gland just below its mouth. This sticky substance is the cause of the silvery trail left behind the snail as it wanders about, and it helps it to climb walls and plant stems. Although usually a slow mover, a snail can take around an hour to cover about 50 metres, if the ground surface is not too rough.

Snails feed on any plant material such as leaves, vegetables and flowers, and even on dead animal material and waste. Food can be stored in its crop, to be digested at a later time.

Snails breathe through a pore — a small opening — located just forward of the shell.

The snail's eyes are at the ends of the long tentacles, and the smaller tentacles help it detect the scents of possible food and to examine its surroundings. The snail's eyesight is very poor; the eyes can't focus, and they can't detect colour. They can see just enough to make out nearby shapes and to distinguish light and dark.

If attacked by a predator, the snail can withdraw its entire body into the shell, but this is no defence against a song thrush. This bird has learned to carry off a snail and drop it onto rocks or bash it against a hard surface to break the shell, and allow it to get to the animal inside.

Snails will lay a cluster of tiny 3-millimetre eggs in the soil, after mating. The young snails emerge from the eggs already bearing delicate, transparent shells. The growing shell must be strengthened with calcium as it develops, and the young snail usually eats its own egg to begin with.

Most garden snails can live for 2 to 3 years.

The great majority of garden and other snails have shells growing to the right of the body (called 'dextral'), as in the small illustration at the top of the page, and a very rare few have shells growing to the left (called 'sinistral'). Because the reproductive organs are reversed in a 'leftie', it's almost impossible for it to mate with a 'rightie', so it may take quite a long time for it to find a suitable mate, even if a snail dating app was available.

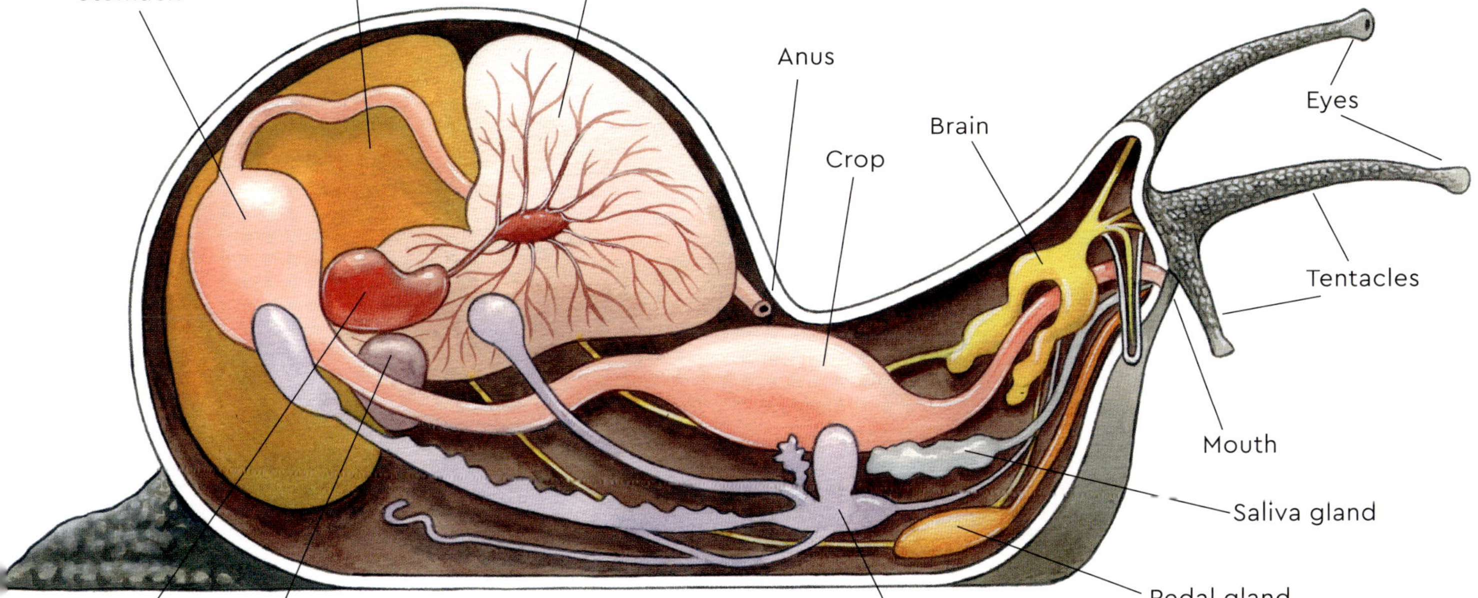

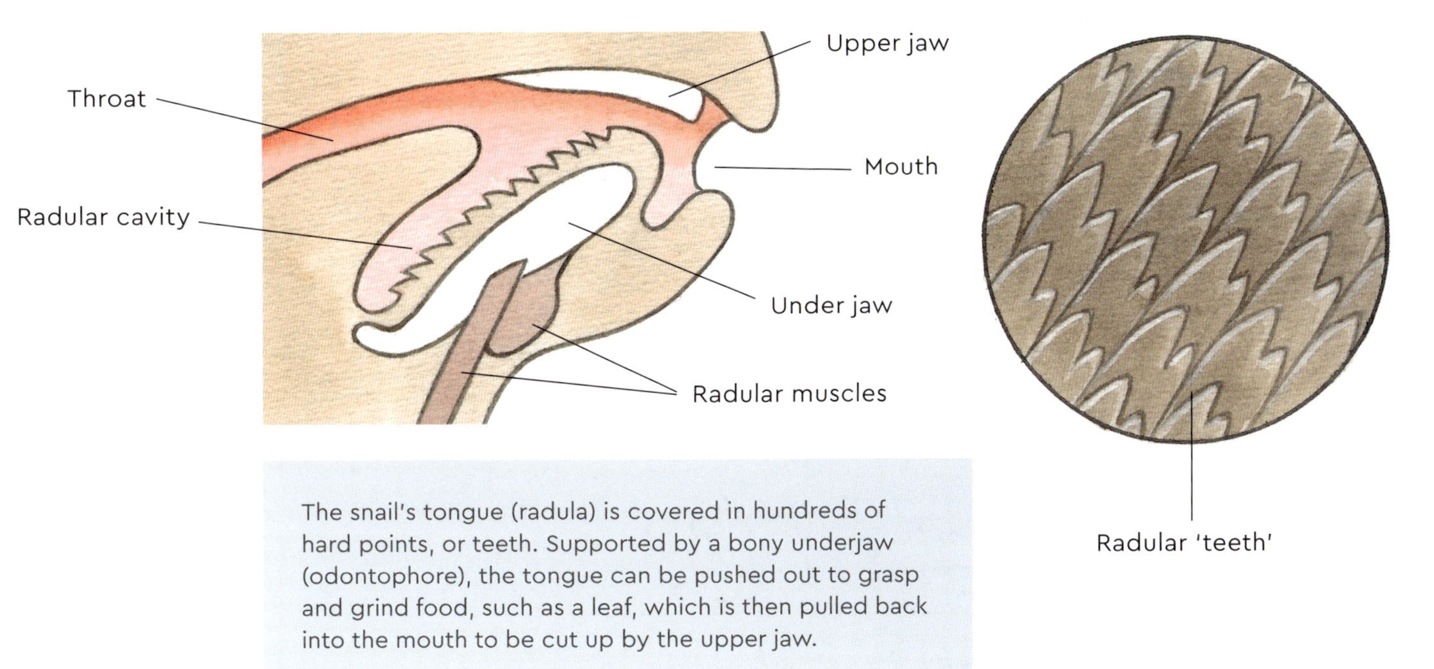

The snail's tongue (radula) is covered in hundreds of hard points, or teeth. Supported by a bony underjaw (odontophore), the tongue can be pushed out to grasp and grind food, such as a leaf, which is then pulled back into the mouth to be cut up by the upper jaw.

Common cockle | tuangi

These small cockles — about 20 to 25 millimetres across — are very common around the shallow waters of New Zealand's sandy and muddy coasts, usually buried just under the surface.

They are bivalve molluscs, which means that they have two hard shells, or valves, with the animal living inside. The two halves are hinged, so that the cockle can open them slightly using strong adductor muscles, and it can then extend a muscular foot to move about.

The cockle feeds by drawing water in through a siphon at the edge of a protective mantle, and the gills filter out tiny food particles, which are then taken up by its mouth and digested, with waste passed out through the anus. The water is expelled through the outward siphon. The cockle doesn't have a true brain but has a very simple nervous system that mostly controls the muscles, foot and other organs.

If attacked by predators such as birds, fish, sea stars or other, larger shellfish, the cockle can close the valves tightly together. However, some birds have learned that they can drop the cockle from a height to break the shell.

They are also a favourite food of humans — Māori have long used them as a good food source.

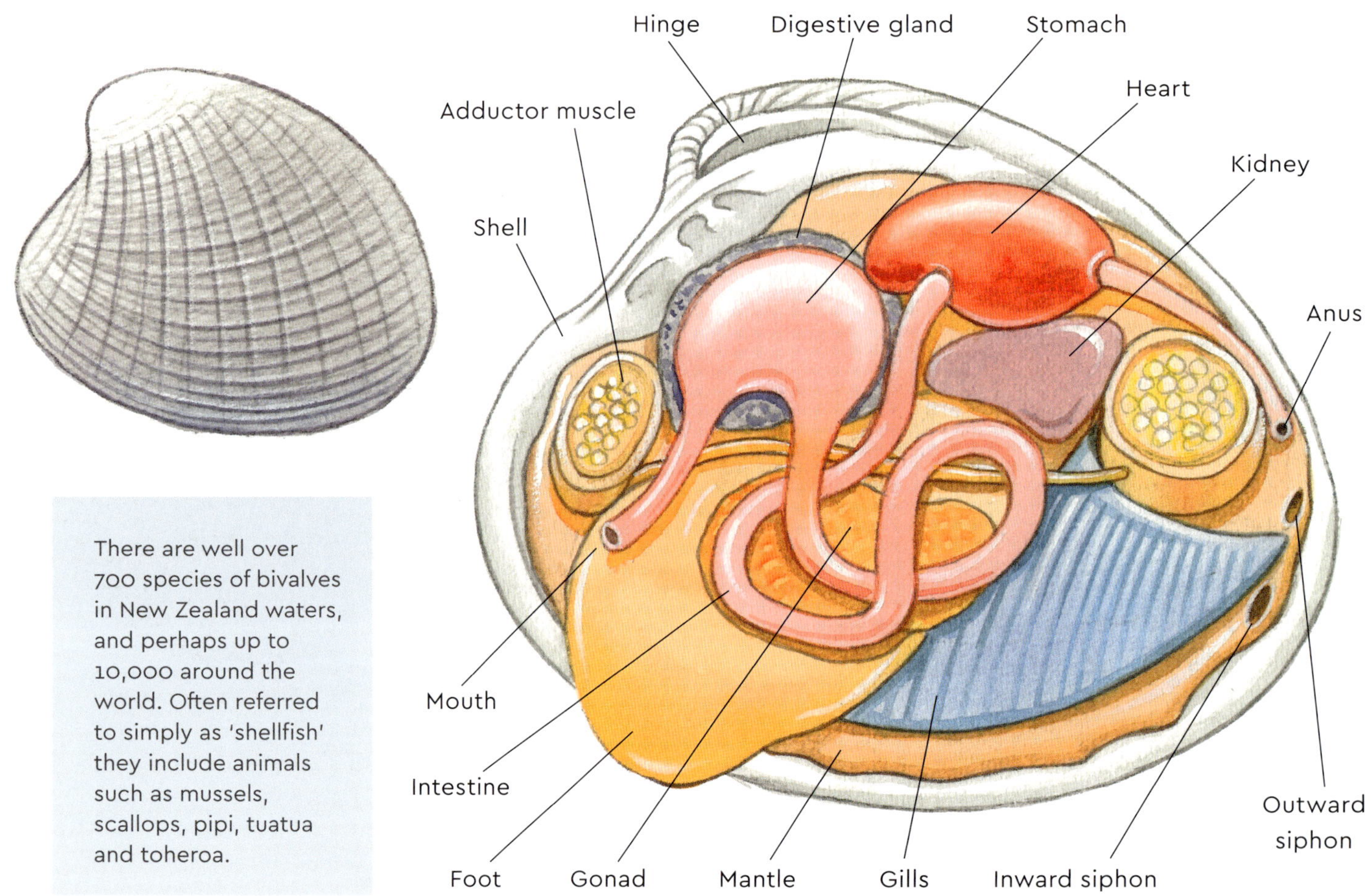

There are well over 700 species of bivalves in New Zealand waters, and perhaps up to 10,000 around the world. Often referred to simply as 'shellfish' they include animals such as mussels, scallops, pipi, tuatua and toheroa.

Common rock crab | pāpaka nui

Crabs belong to a group of animals called Crustacea, which includes crayfish, prawns, shrimps, barnacles and even garden woodlice. All have hard and jointed 'armour' to protect their limbs and bodies. The hard covering protecting the body is called a carapace.

A crab has 10 legs, with the front pair equipped with pincers, which it can use to take food or fend off predators. As a young crab grows, it needs to get rid of its hard covering several times and allow the new, larger one developing underneath to expand and harden.

Part of these cast-off 'moults' are often found around the shore.

The common rock crab — probably named because it's a common crab around seashore rocks! — is one of the most easily seen crabs around New Zealand's rocky shores. It's equally happy in the waters of rockpools or scavenging about on the rocks above. Although it only measures about 4 centimetres across the back, it can be quite aggressive if disturbed — waving its pincers and charging, before running off or retreating quickly into a rocky crevice. Like many shore crabs, the rock crab is a scavenger and will eat just about anything it can get its pincers on — worms, shellfish, other crabs . . . in fact, any plant or animal material, alive or dead, will do. These crabs can live for about 5 years.

There are about 200 crab species in New Zealand, but most live in deeper waters. About 20 or more can be seen around the shores — in rockpools and in shallow waters.

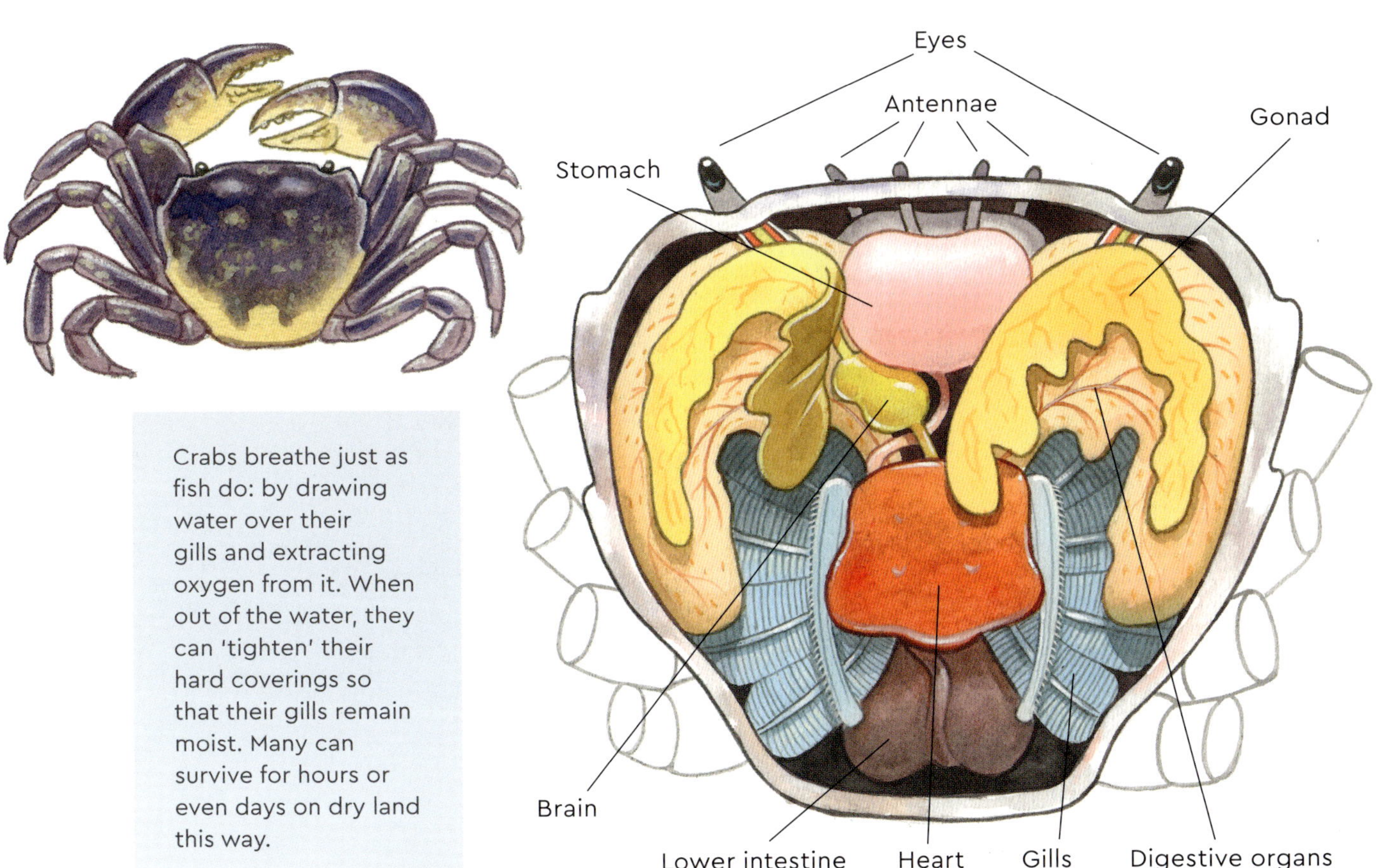

Crabs breathe just as fish do: by drawing water over their gills and extracting oxygen from it. When out of the water, they can 'tighten' their hard coverings so that their gills remain moist. Many can survive for hours or even days on dry land this way.

House-hopper spider | pūngāwerewere

All spiders have two body parts — the forebody (cephalothorax) and the abdomen — and have four pairs of legs. Another pair of 'limbs' — the pedipalps — are used to handle captured prey and to examine surroundings.

Most spiders have four pairs of eyes. They can't move their eyes, as we can, so each pair has a different function: the two front pairs are used for focusing on possible prey and for gauging distance. The pairs around the sides can detect movement and changes in light.

To breathe, air is drawn in through the underside of the abdomen as a spider moves and into the book lung — so called because of its resemblance to stacked pages.

This little jumping spider — just 5 millimetres long — is one of the most commonly seen around the garden and even inside houses. Its eyesight is extremely fine, almost the equal of human sight. It will even react to its own image, if shown a small mirror!

Rather than building webs (although they can) jumping spiders actively hunt prey, such as small insects, by sneaking up and then pouncing in a great leap, just like a cat. The captured prey is then injected with venom from the spider's fangs.

Spiders can eat the victim, or inject digestive fluids into it, reducing the innards to a gooey pulp, which the spider can then suck out, leaving an empty insect husk behind.

The slightly larger flax jumping spider — also called the black-headed jumping spider — can also be seen around the garden and occasionally inside the house.

Both jumpers are quite harmless to humans and will readily jump on and off a human hand, while exploring their surroundings.

There are about 150 species of jumping spiders in New Zealand, and most can live for 1 to 2 years.

Some jumping spiders can jump more than 30 times their own body length.

They always trail a fine line of silk from their spinnerets, so that if they miss their target and fall, they can climb back up (eating the silk line as they do so) and try once more.

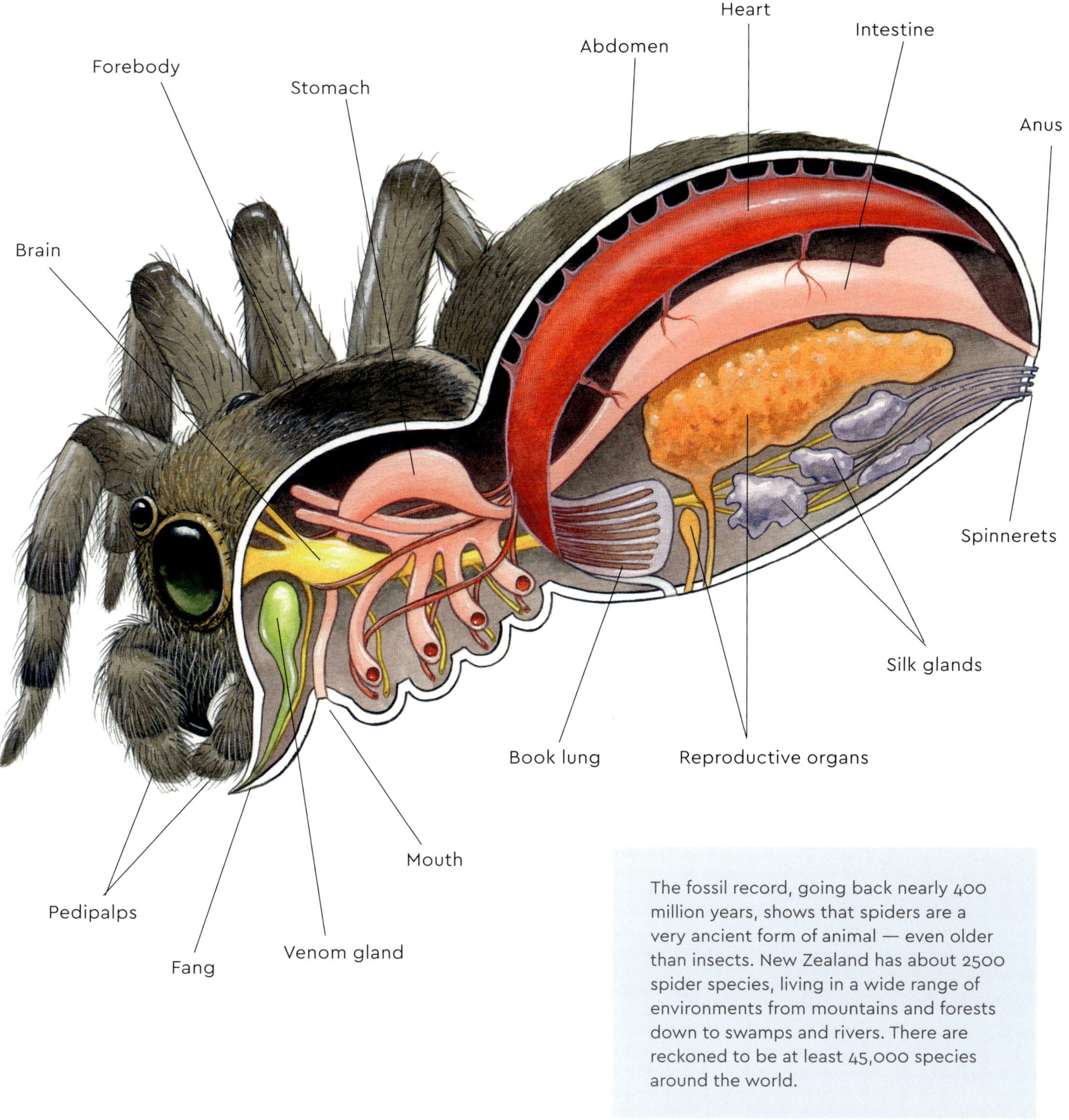

The fossil record, going back nearly 400 million years, shows that spiders are a very ancient form of animal — even older than insects. New Zealand has about 2500 spider species, living in a wide range of environments from mountains and forests down to swamps and rivers. There are reckoned to be at least 45,000 species around the world.

More than a million species of insects have been found so far, making them the most diverse form of animal on Earth. Experts think that there could be as many as 30 million more different types yet to be found.

Insects evolved from some of the very first creatures to move from the sea to the land, hundreds of millions of years ago.

Bumblebee | pī rorohū

Like all other insects, the bumblebee's body is divided into three distinct parts — head (with eyes, antennae and mouth), thorax (middle section, with three pairs of legs) and abdomen (rear section, with most digestive, circulatory and reproductive organs). Many insects have a pair of wings, or two pairs, like the bumblebee.

There are several species of bumblebee in New Zealand, and about 250 known around the world. They were first brought here in 1885 from England to help pollinate clover plant flowers growing in Christchurch, as the tongues of the earlier introduced honeybees were found to be too short.

Unlike the packed and ordered hives of the honeybee, the bumblebee lives in small colonies with populations numbering no more than a few hundred. They don't build large combs of honey, but instead store food in small waxy 'pots'.

Bumblebee honey is quite different from that made by honeybees — it's made from a combination of plant pollen and the bee's own saliva, and it is stored in a separate part of its stomach, called a honey crop, until needed. Plant pollen is also used to make food, and it's gathered and stored on the sides of the bee's hind legs, as it journeys from plant to plant to suck up nectar from deep inside each flower with its long extendable tongue. A busy bee can visit up to 400 flowers in an hour — see also the kōwhai flower on page 9. As it lands on each flower, the bee's feet leave a telltale smell behind, which tells other bees that the flower has already been visited — and the smell then fades away in roughly the same time as the flower replaces the nectar in its base.

Although the bumblebee can bite, with its small jaws (mandibles), it feels like no more than a tickle on human skin. Some bees will use their jaws to cut through the underside of a flower that might be too long and deep for them to reach the nectar in the normal way.

The bumblebee's sting is a far more effective weapon. The honeybee's sting is barbed along its side, and so while it can sting another insect several times, the sting gets stuck in tougher human skin, and gets pulled out of the bee's body as it flies off. As the bumblebee's sting is smooth, it doesn't lodge in the skin, so the bumblebee can sting several times. Fortunately, the bumblebee is much less aggressive than the honeybee.

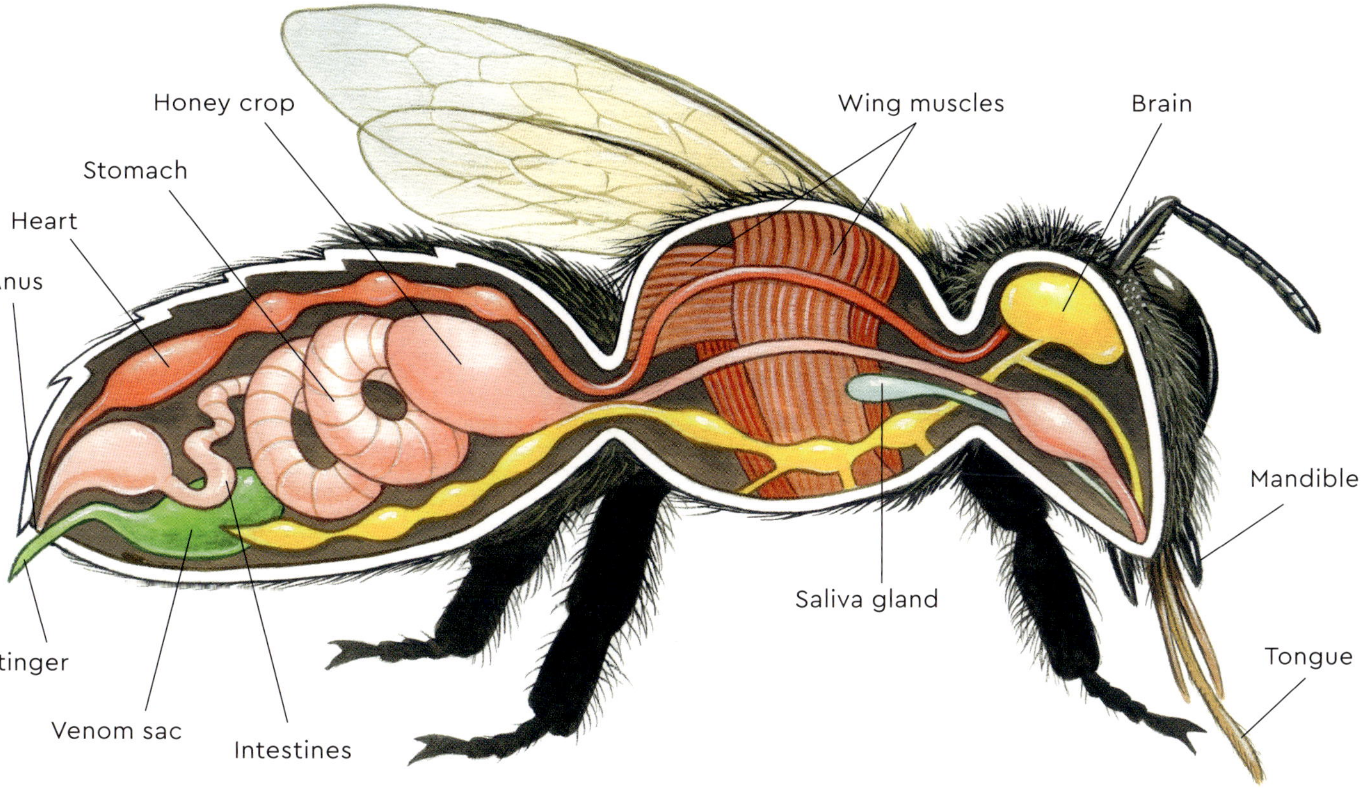

Honey crop
Wing muscles
Brain
Stomach
Heart
Anus
Mandible
Saliva gland
Tongue
Stinger
Venom sac
Intestines

Compound eye

Like the bumblebee and other insects, crabs and some other arthropods have a pair of compound eyes. This means that instead of having an eye with a single lens, as we do, the eye is divided into hundreds or even tens of thousands of individual lenses. Each individual lens can focus light and has pigment cells for detecting colour. These lenses combine to form a single image in the insect's brain — not a multitude, as is sometimes believed. Many insects have a much greater range of vision than other animals, which is one reason why it's hard to sneak up on a fly to swat it — it can *always* see you coming!

Cornea
Lens
Receptor cells
Pigment cells

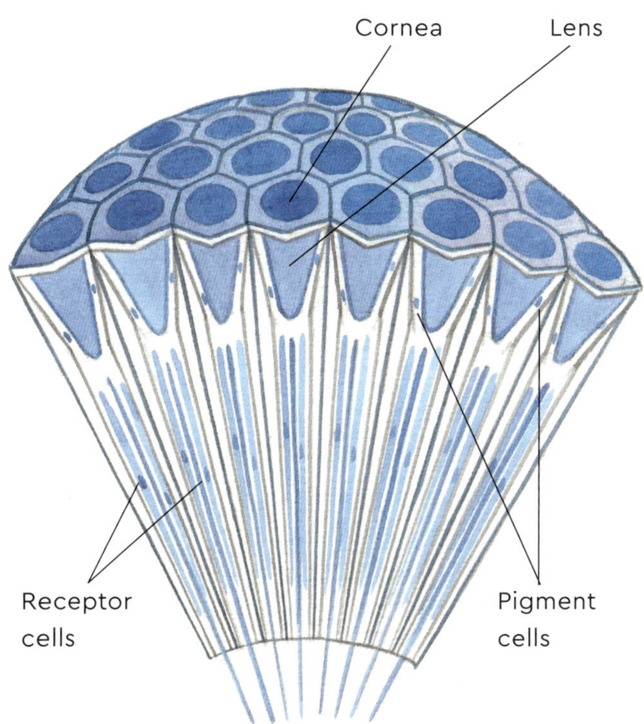

The Māori name of wētā comes from wētāpunga, which means 'God of ugly things' and one of its scientific names — *Deinacrida* — means 'terrible grasshopper'.

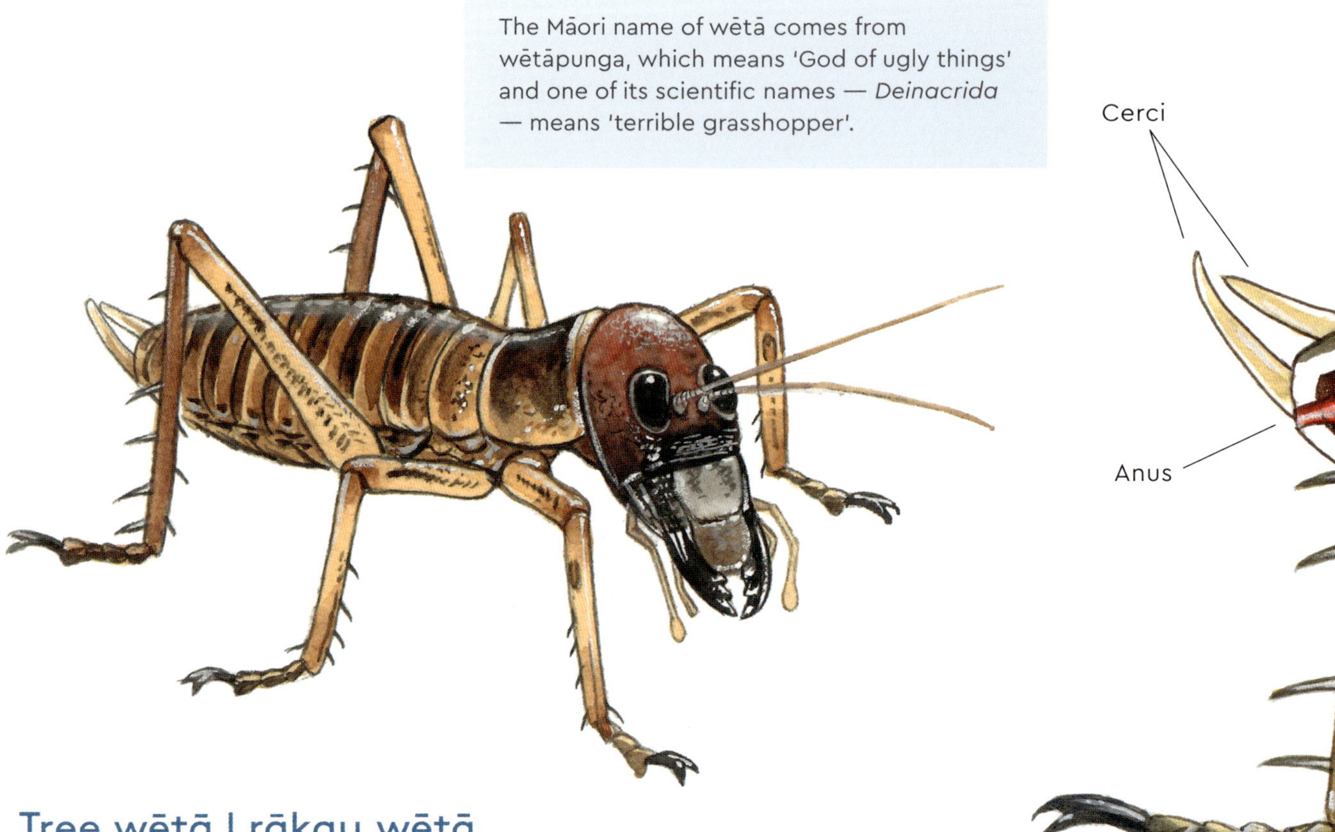

Tree wētā | rākau wētā

The 7 centimetre-long tree wētā is the most commonly seen member of the wētā family, and it can be found in forests and gardens throughout most of the country.

Wētā are mostly active at night, when they roam about to catch small insects and chew on new plant growth. If disturbed by a predator, such as a bird or rat, the wētā can scratch with the spines on its long hind legs, or give a sharp bite with its very strong mandibles (jaws). Much of the inside of the wētā's head is actually taken up by the jaw muscles.

Tree wētā will often occupy holes in old trees or fallen logs or in the gaps in stacks of firewood. Going in head first, they can defend their homes by raising their hind legs to present the sharp spines to any intruder. The palps around the jaws are sensors for smell and taste, and the discs on the wētā's front legs are actually its ears.

Like other insects, the wētā has no lungs, but breathes through a series of spiracles (fine holes) set along the abdomen. Oxygen is then distributed throughout the body through fine trachea (tubes).

Males have a larger head than the females and have projections called cerci (sensory feelers) at the rear of the abdomen. The long spike at the rear of the female's abdomen is not a sting but an ovipositor, which she uses to lay her eggs in damp soil or rotten tree bark.

There are about seven species of tree wētā, and most live for about 8 to 10 years.

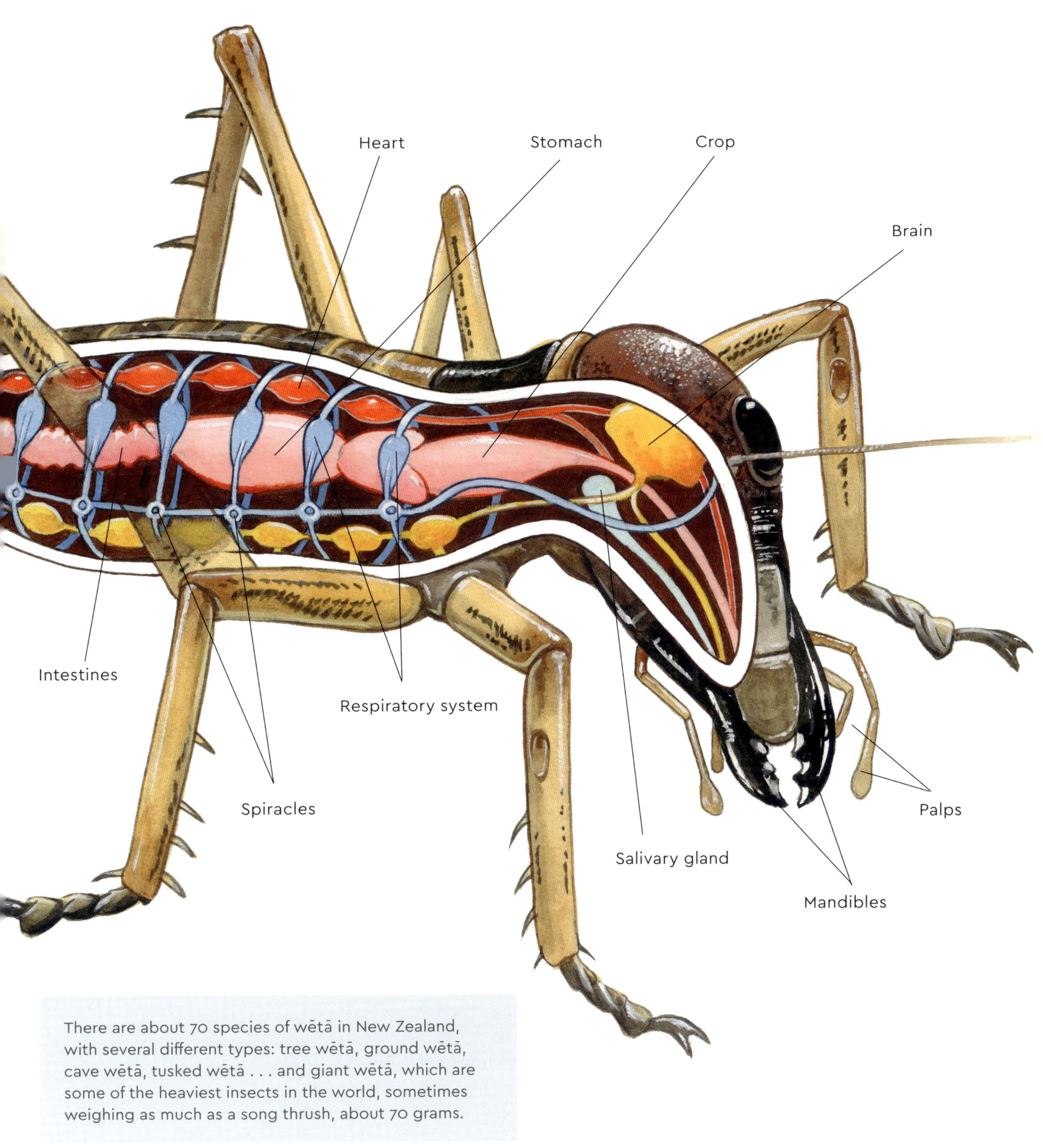

There are about 70 species of wētā in New Zealand, with several different types: tree wētā, ground wētā, cave wētā, tusked wētā . . . and giant wētā, which are some of the heaviest insects in the world, sometimes weighing as much as a song thrush, about 70 grams.

Ant | pōpokorua

While ants follow the standard insect body arrangement of head, thorax and abdomen, they have an extra body segment called a petiole. This acts as a flexible joint, and it allows the ant to swing its abdomen forward, to use its venom-loaded stinger (although not all species have stingers) or to spray acid to defend itself or to attack prey.

They also have trail glands. Ants out foraging for food leave a 'smell trail' as they travel. Other ants follow the trail back and forth, if food is discovered, and the trail is strengthened. As the food reduces, so less workers use the trail, and the scent eventually fades away.

An ant's sense of smell is very strong. A small drop of jam, or some sugar, left on a kitchen bench, will soon attract an investigating ant or two . . . and quickly followed by a line of them going backwards and forwards.

Ants don't have front 'grasping' legs, as many other ground insects do, so their mandibles (jaws) have a lot of work to do — they can dig, crush, grip, cut and hold and even clean themselves and other ants with their mandibles.

Ants usually live in large underground colonies, which can number anywhere between a few hundred individuals up to a million or more. A colony is ruled by a single queen ant, who lays eggs to create new colony members. The workers ants can live for about 2 to 3 years, and the queen can live for 20 years or more.

There are about 40 ant species in New Zealand, with about 20,000 species known around the world. Most ants measure about 2 to 5 millimetres in length.

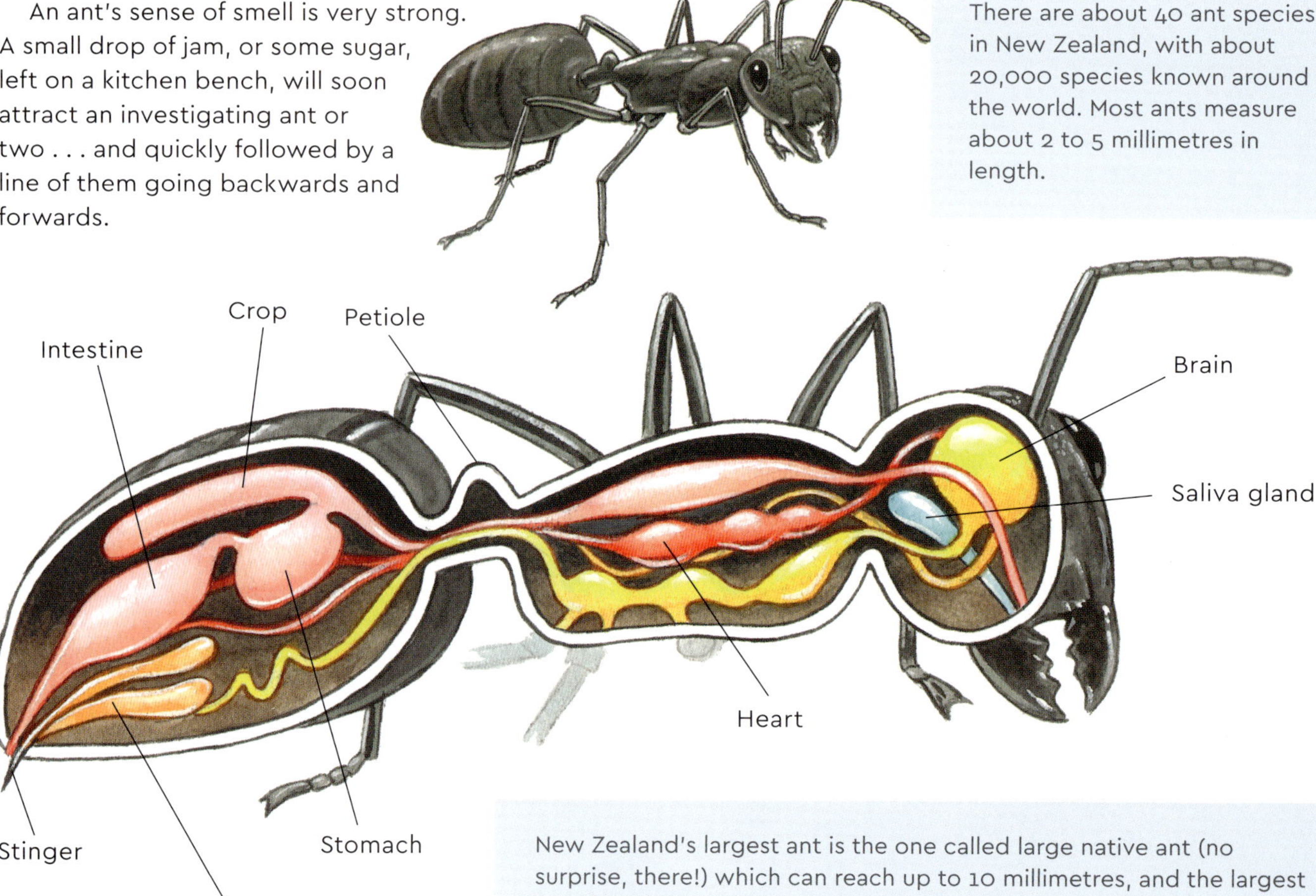

New Zealand's largest ant is the one called large native ant (no surprise, there!) which can reach up to 10 millimetres, and the largest ants in the world can measure nearly 3 centimetres in length.

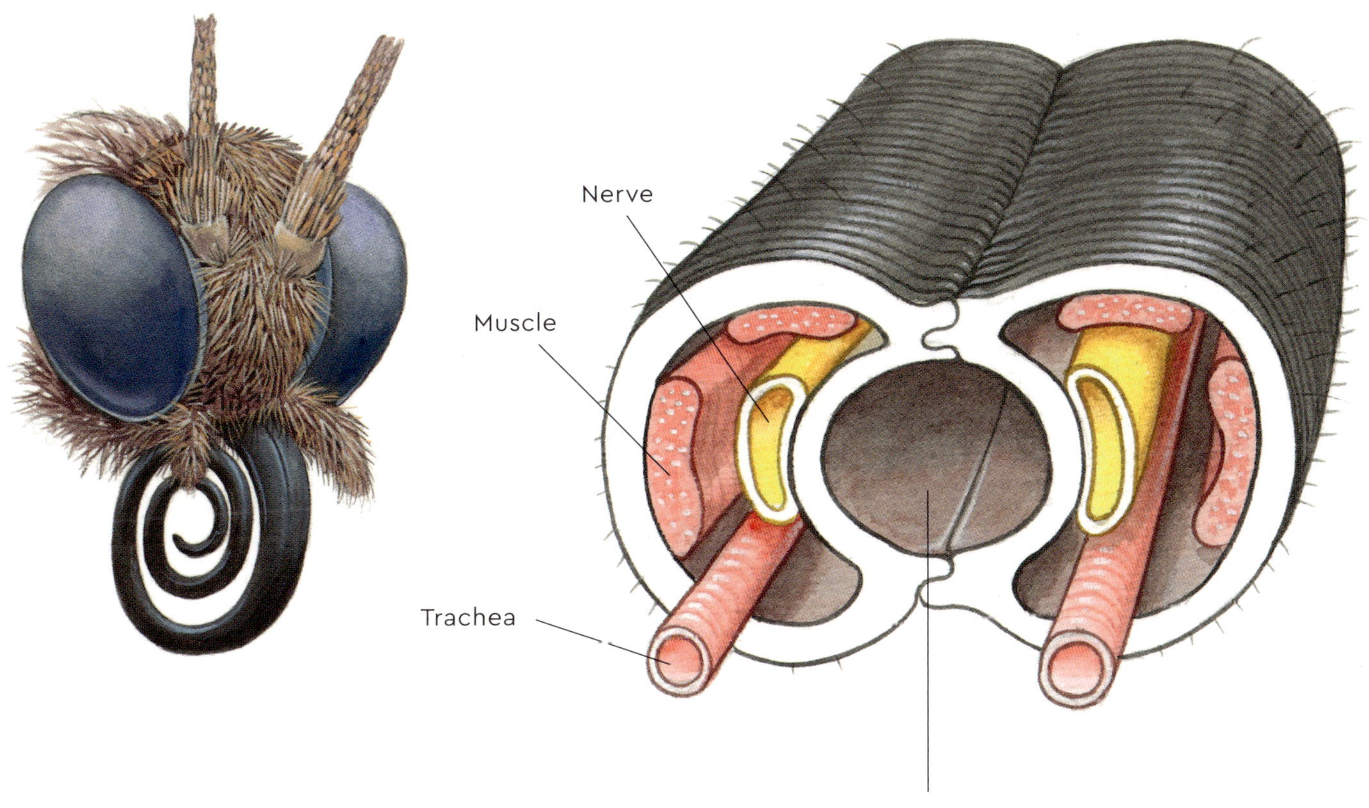

How butterflies feed

Nearly all insects have mouth openings and 'jaws' of some kind, with parts that may resemble cutting pincers, lips and even tongues. However, the great majority of butterflies and moths have a proboscis instead of a proper mouth. This is in effect a simple tube, which can be unfurled and straightened so that the insect can suck up nectar from inside a flower, or water and the juices from fruits. Some butterflies prefer to take up tree sap, or even rotting plant or animal material.

When a butterfly emerges from a chrysalis, the proboscis is in two halves, and by coiling and uncurling it, and with plenty of saliva added, the butterfly gradually 'stitches' the two halves together, to form one long 'drinking straw'. If the two halves become separated later through accident, most butterflies can repair and reassemble the proboscis.

At the end of each of its six legs are taste organs that the butterfly uses to find food. When a butterfly's leg touches a good food source, a reflex causes its proboscis to uncoil. This lets the butterfly draw and suck up and swallow the food, which is digested in organs in the butterfly's abdomen.

Inside the proboscis are nerves, trachea — which carry oxygen from its lungs — and muscles which control its movement and curling. And at the centre is, of course, the feeding canal.

Bronze whaler shark | horopekapeka

The bronze whaler is one of the most common sharks to be seen in New Zealand's coastal waters. They will often venture into the shallow waters of beaches and bays all around the North Island, especially in summer; gliding past swimmers and surfers as they hunt for fish, such as kahawai.

Although they usually measure 1.5 to 2.5 metres in length, some can reach over 3 metres.

Sharks — and rays — are known as 'cartilaginous' fish, as their bones are made of a lighter material than that found in 'bony' fish, such as the snapper on page 30. This cartilage is similar to the material that gives shape and strength to human noses and ears. A shark's skeleton will quickly decay after death, but the jaws — made of a denser cartilage — are substantial and strong enough to survive.

The shark's skeleton is much reduced, when compared to that of a bony fish — consisting of a skull, jaws, backbone, support structures for the gills, and a series of cartilaginous 'rods' which strengthen and hold the shape of the fins and tail.

The jaw is quite separate from the skull, which means that the shark can actually thrust it forward into a larger gape when biting into prey.

The lateral line of the shark's side is sensitive to vibrations in the water, and its snout is covered in tiny gel-filled pores called ampullae of Lorenzini — these can detect the electrical fields generated by fish and others at great distances, even over many tens of kilometres. These aids mean that sharks can easily detect prey hiding under the sand of the seabed, or far away beyond their eyesight, or in the dark.

Shark skin is quite different from that of the bony fish. It's rough, like fine sandpaper, and made up from countless tiny 'denticles' — sharp teeth-like points supported and anchored within the skin by small pieces of cartilage. This rough skin helps to decrease drag in the water and allows the shark to swim quietly and fast.

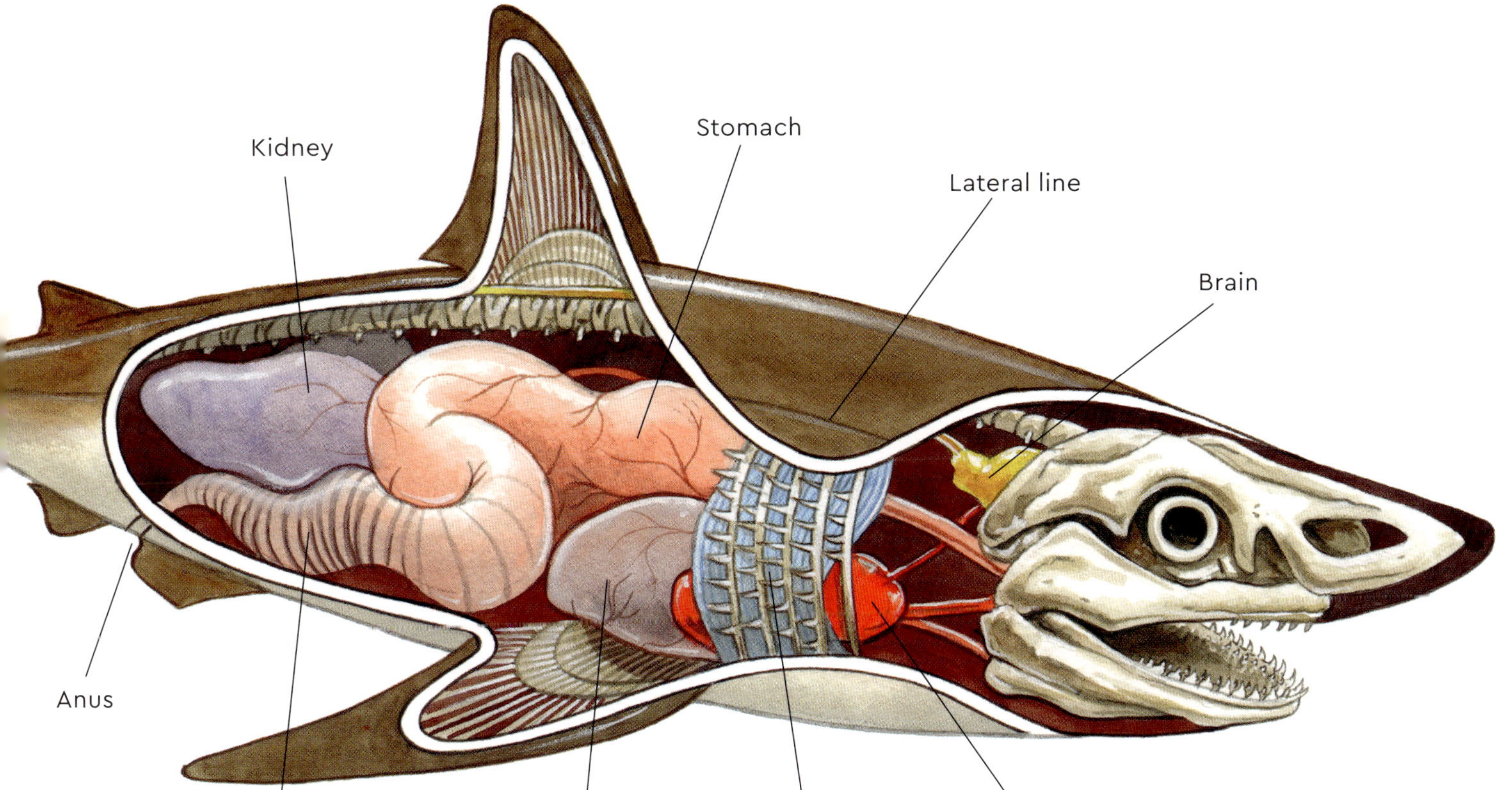

Kidney
Stomach
Lateral line
Brain
Anus
Intestine
Liver
Gills
Heart

The bronze whaler usually has more than 60 teeth, measuring up to 30 millimetres in length. The teeth are set in an internal 'conveyor belt'; as the front teeth wear away or break off, so the next row moves forward, with more teeth emerging behind. Shark teeth have no roots, as mammals' do, so they are easily broken off. Some shark species may have up to 15 rows of teeth in various stages of development.

Developing teeth
Older teeth discarded
Lower jaw

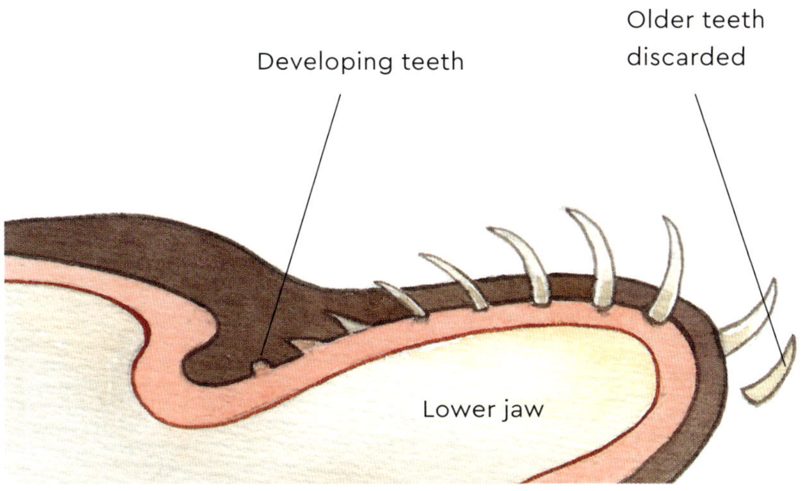

Snapper | tāmure

Snapper are one of our most abundant fish, and they can be found around much of the North Island's coastal waters and the upper half of the South Island.

They are an important part of New Zealand's fishing industry and have been a significant part of Māori kaimoana for hundreds of years.

Besides their usual habitats of reefs and shallow seas, these fish will enter estuaries and harbours to hunt for prey such as sea stars, small fish and crabs. They are particularly fond of shellfish and kina, and their strong and impressive jaws and teeth can make short work of any hard shell to get at the animal inside . . . and they're powerful enough to crush an inquisitive diver's finger, too.

They are what is known as a 'bony' fish, in that they have a substantial and complete skeleton which will not readily decay after death — as opposed to the incomplete and friable nature of a shark's skeleton (see previous pages). Bony fish such as snapper have proper overlapping scales covering their body, and have a single gill opening, while most cartilaginous fish — sharks and rays — have five.

When very young and small, snapper mostly keep to protective places like kelp forests and seagrass meadows rather than open water, where there are plenty of predators, such as sharks. They are also prey for shorebirds and fish such as kahawai and John Dory. Even adult snapper will hunt the youngsters.

Like many fish species, young snapper are all born female, but when they reach the first stages of maturity, after 3 to 4 years, about half of them will develop into males.

They are quite long-living fish; some may even reach an age of 60 years. Often called 'old man snapper', these veterans can grow up to 1.3 metres in length and weigh 20 kilograms or more.

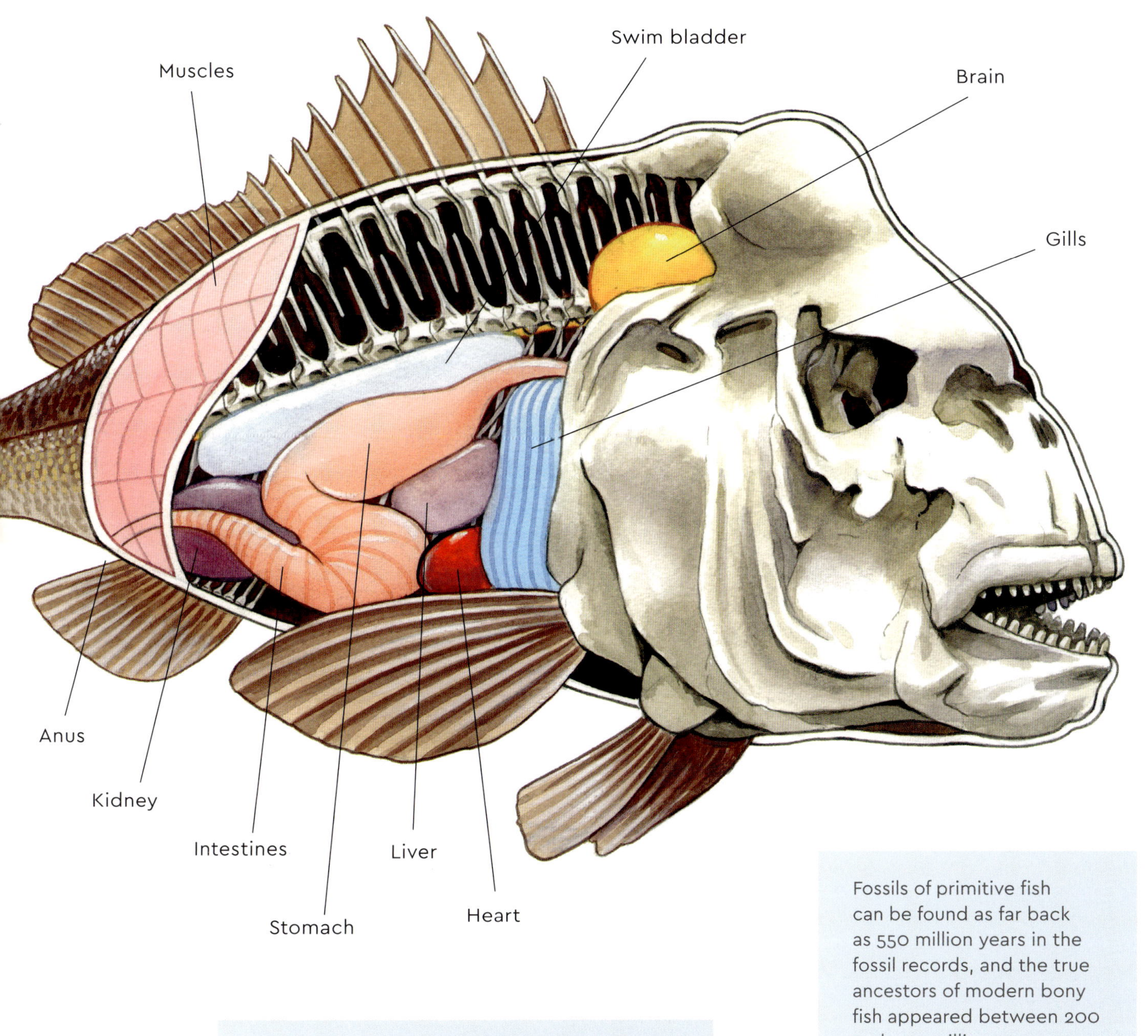

Fossils of primitive fish can be found as far back as 550 million years in the fossil records, and the true ancestors of modern bony fish appeared between 200 and 400 million years ago.

There are over 29,000 species of fish known, and about 96 per cent of these are bony fish — making them the largest group of invertebrates (animals with backbones) known.

Frogs belong to a class of animals called amphibians. This includes frogs, salamanders and others. All live in or near water, and most young have gills to let them breathe while in the water, and they then develop lungs so they can live on land. Some species lack proper lungs and can breathe through their skin. There are about 8000 species of amphibians, and nearly 90 per cent of them are frogs.

Hochstetter's frogs do not have a free-swimming tadpole stage as other more common and 'modern' frogs do — the tadpole stage takes place inside the egg, and then tiny frogs emerge as they hatch.

Hochstetter's frog | pepeketua

All four of New Zealand's native frogs are quite primitive in nature — they have remained practically unchanged in fossil evidence for at least 70 million years.

Hochstetter's frogs live near streams in a few small forest locations in the northern half of the North Island. By day, they rest in cool, damp places such as under logs or stones close to the water. At night, they come out to feed. Lacking the long extensible tongue of many frogs, they simply snatch up small insects and spiders from the forest floor.

They also differ from other frogs in that they lack external eardrums, and so they do not 'call' — there's no point in saying 'ribbit' when other frogs cannot hear it!

However, if disturbed, a Hochstetter's frog might yelp or chirp its displeasure.

They do have good eyesight and can also recognise other frogs by chemical signals.

Despite their diminutive size — the illustration at top is at life size — Hochstetter's frogs can live for about 30 years.

The smallest amphibian — and also the smallest animal with a proper skeleton — is a New Guinea frog that measures just 7.7 millimetres in length. The largest amphibian is the South China giant salamander, which can measure up to 1.8 metres.

Green turtle | honu

Green turtles are quite common in the seas around northern parts of New Zealand. While they will eat fish, sponges, jellyfish and shellfish, they are the only sea turtle species to feed on marine plants, such as seagrasses, seaweeds and even mangroves. Because of this plant-rich diet, the turtles' body fat has a greenish tinge, which gives the turtle its name, not the colour of its shell — which is more often seen to be brown, rather than green.

As it grows, the turtle develops wide, expanded ribs, with a hard shell covering, called a carapace. The underside — called a plastron — is similarly protected with expanded bony plates.

Although vulnerable while small and growing, the adult turtle's tough skeleton makes it a difficult meal for all but the largest predator, such as sharks . . . and humans.

They are usually leisurely swimmers, but if chasing fish or escaping predators, they can reach speeds up to 35 kilometres per hour using their large, powerful flippers.

Green turtles are one of the largest types of hard-shelled sea turtles, and they can weigh over 150 kilograms, with a carapace measuring about 1 metre in length. They can live for 80 years or more.

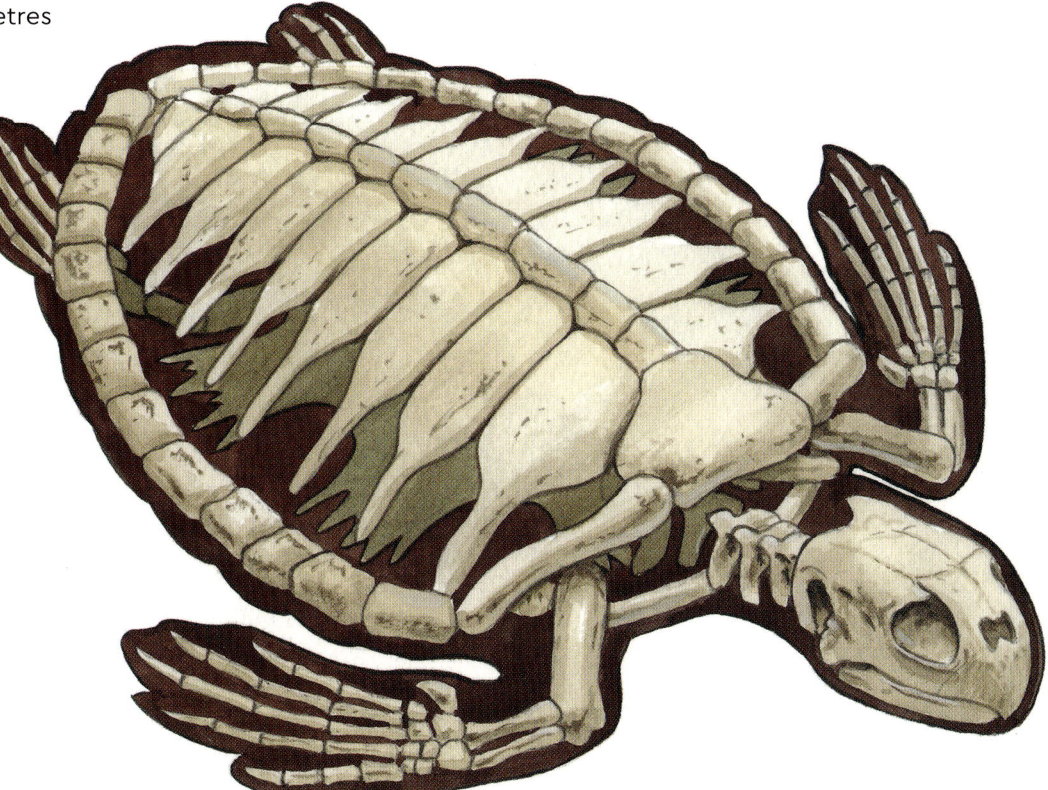

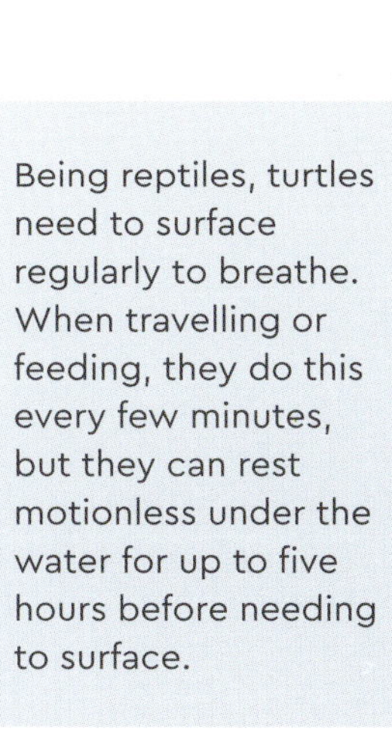

Being reptiles, turtles need to surface regularly to breathe. When travelling or feeding, they do this every few minutes, but they can rest motionless under the water for up to five hours before needing to surface.

Tuatara

The tuatara has no close relatives. Reptiles are divided into just four groups: crocodiles and alligators, lizards and snakes, turtles and tortoises, and all by itself in the fourth group is the tuatara.

Although sometimes referred to as a 'living fossil' the tuatara is actually one of the most successful animal species — it has remained practically unchanged for around 200 million years and has managed to survive the extinctions which killed off the dinosaurs, many small and large ice ages, and other extremes of weather and climate.

Once common throughout New Zealand, tuatara are now mostly confined to offshore islands, because of predation by introduced rats, dogs and pigs.

There are two species — the main tuatara species numbers in the thousands, while the subspecies called Gunther's tuatara has only some hundreds of individuals.

They live in long, deep burrows, often sharing it with a seabird such as a shearwater. They roam at night to catch and feed on prey such as wētā, beetles, skinks and geckos. They may even take one or two of the shearwater's eggs or chicks if they're especially hungry.

Tuatara possess a third eye — called a parietal eye — under the skin on the top of the head. Although it has a lens and a simple cornea, this eye cannot 'see' in the normal sense. It can detect light and dark, and it may help the tuatara to absorb ultraviolet rays to produce vitamin D and help with regulating its body temperature. Tuatara will sometimes come to the entrance of their burrow to 'sunbathe'.

Tuatara have primitive but very efficient teeth. The single row on the lower jaw can interlock with a double row of teeth in the upper jaw, and the tuatara can then move its jaw forward to shear through the bones of its prey.

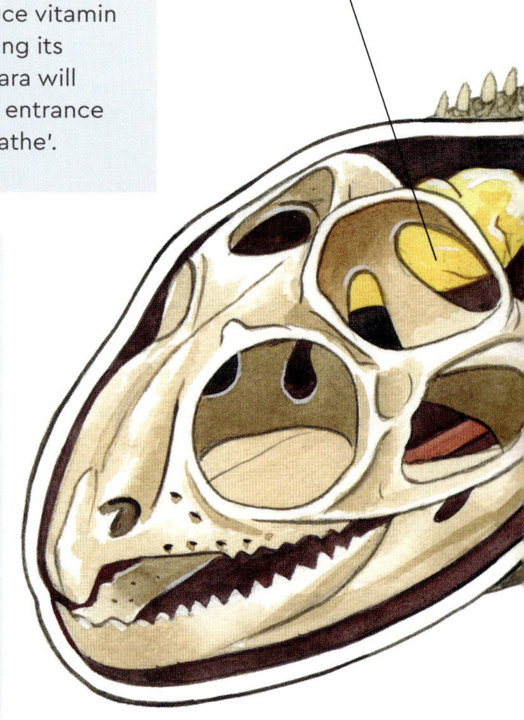

The spines running along the tuatara's back are soft, not rigid — the Māori name tuatara means 'spiny back' or 'peaks on the back'.

Male tuatara are larger than females and can weigh from 500 grams to well over 1 kilogram.

Larger tuatara can measure around 60 centimetres from their snout to the tip of their tail. They have a long life span, too: up to 100 years or more.

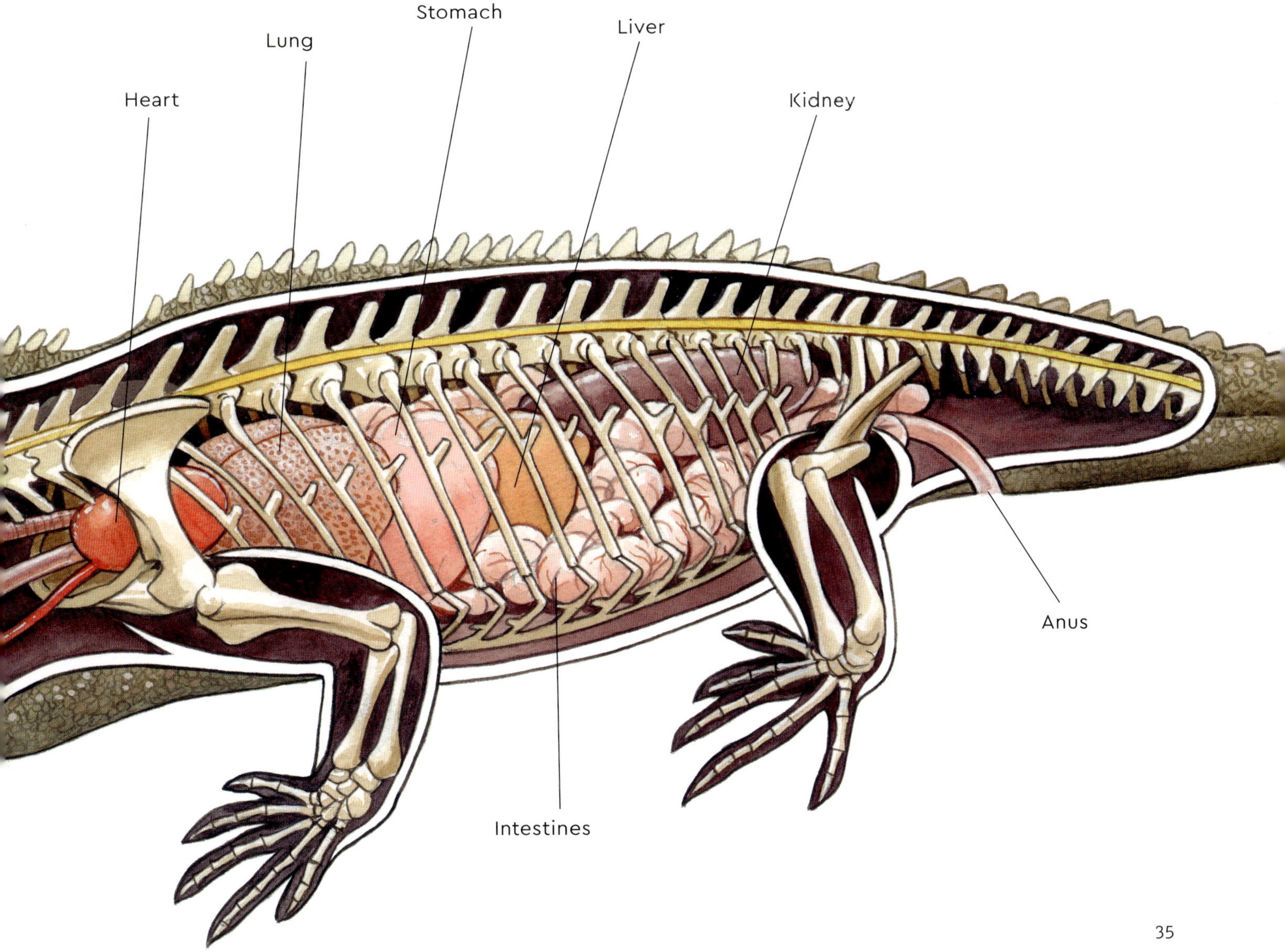

Stomach
Lung
Liver
Heart
Kidney
Anus
Intestines

Kiwi

If any animal can claim to be our national symbol, it has to be the kiwi.

There are actually five kiwi species. The brown kiwi (rowi), found in the upper South Island; Southern brown kiwi (tokoeka), in the lower South Island and Stewart Island; the great spotted kiwi (roroa) from the South Island; and the little spotted kiwi (kiwi pukupuku), found in both main islands.

The most common is the brown kiwi, found in a wide range of habitats throughout the country, but mostly in the upper North Island. Brown kiwi usually weigh about 2.2 to 2.8 kilograms and are about 40 to 50 centimetres long — including the bill. They can live for up to about 20 to 30 years.

All the species of kiwi once numbered in the millions, but introduced predators — rats, stoats and dogs — and the clearing of forests have drastically reduced their populations.

All kiwi make their nests in deep burrows, and only emerge at dusk to forage about on the forest floor, digging through leaf litter and into the ground with their long bills. Their nostrils are located near the tip of the bill, so the kiwi can smell possible prey as they poke into the earth. They will feed on fallen fruits, insects, spiders, worms and grubs.

The birds' name simply comes from the call of the male kiwi as it leaves its burrow at night . . . *ki-weeee*. The female's call is more like a hoarse shriek.

As they are flightless, their bones have evolved to be much more dense and heavier than that of birds who fly. The large keel breastbone of flying birds — essential for anchoring the muscles for the wings — has been reduced to a small bony plate. Compare the 'chest' bones of the kiwi to that of the fantail (page 39) and the penguin (page 41). Kiwi have strong, muscled legs with sharp talons (their legs can account for about a third of the bird's total body weight). They will use these talons and their long bills as weapons to fight other kiwi — or possible predators — who have entered a kiwi's home territory, which can be anything between 2 and 40 hectares in size.

Even though part of its scientific name — *Apteryx* — comes from the Greek, and means 'no wing,' the kiwi does have wings. As it adopted a ground-foraging lifestyle over time, the wings gradually became reduced in size, to become just simple limbs with a single claw — small enough to always remain hidden under the bird's rough feathers. It makes for a handy spot for the kiwi to tuck in its bill when it curls up to sleep.

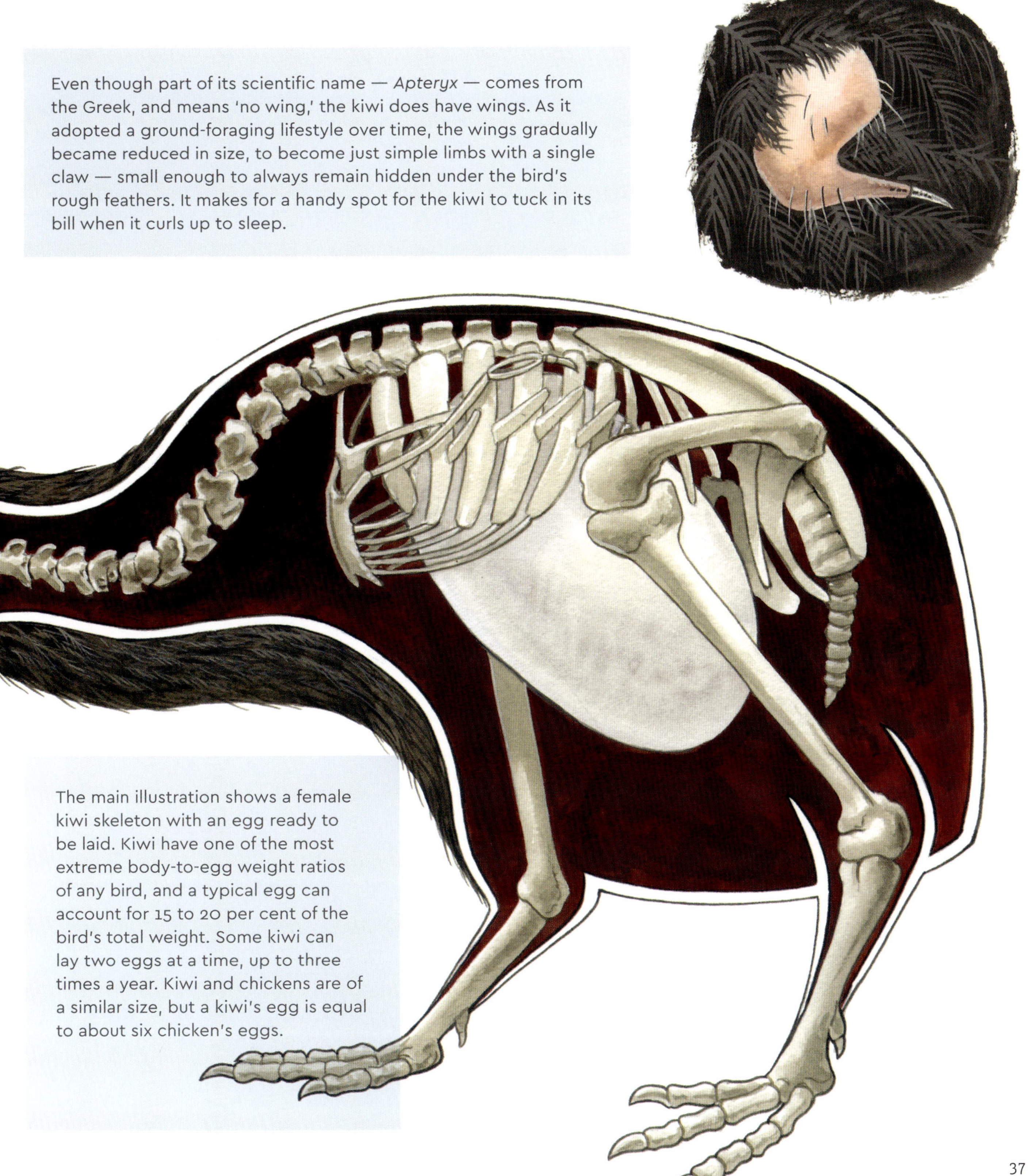

The main illustration shows a female kiwi skeleton with an egg ready to be laid. Kiwi have one of the most extreme body-to-egg weight ratios of any bird, and a typical egg can account for 15 to 20 per cent of the bird's total weight. Some kiwi can lay two eggs at a time, up to three times a year. Kiwi and chickens are of a similar size, but a kiwi's egg is equal to about six chicken's eggs.

Fantails can be found throughout the country, with slightly different forms, depending on the region — some all-black fantails can be seen in the South Island and in the Wellington region. They usually live for about 3 to 10 years.

Fantail | pīwakawaka

This little bird's name is well-deserved, as its long tail can be spread as a fan in an instant, and allow it to 'brake' in mid-flight, and change direction quickly. Being such a quick and agile flyer, the fantail will often follow humans on forest walks, to snatch up any insects that they might disturb. It rarely feeds on the ground but will sometimes hover in flight to take beetles or spiders from branches and leaves.

The most important part of a flying bird's 'engine' are the primary and secondary flight feathers. These feathers are anchored to the bird's wing bones — the primary feathers are attached to the bird's 'hand' and 'finger' bones, and the secondary feathers are attached to the forearm (see also Forearm homology, page 43). The large keel bone in the bird's chest provides an anchor for the powerful muscles of the wing bones. In flightless birds, of course, the keel is not so essential, and is much reduced in size — see the kiwi skeleton on the previous pages.

All the feathers overlap slightly, and the secondary feathers cover the primaries when the wing is folded. The flight feathers are overlaid above and below by further layers of feathers to provide a solid and smoothly streamlined surface for flight. Each individual 'hair' (barbule) along the stem of a wing feather has tiny hooks along its length, which allows it to lock with its neighbour, and so keeps out water and wind. Tail feathers have a similar structure and can be manoeuvred to provide accurate steering in flight.

There are several layers of small feathers covering the bird's body — with the 'fluffiest' ones closest to the skin, and the outermost ones similar in structure to the large wing feathers. These layered feathers provide good insulation and help the bird to retain body warmth. The simplest feathers of all are the short bristles around the base of the bill, where they help to protect the bird's face and eyes.

If a number of the flight feathers are lost or clipped — despite any furious flapping — the bird simply cannot achieve the 'lift' required to take off into the air.

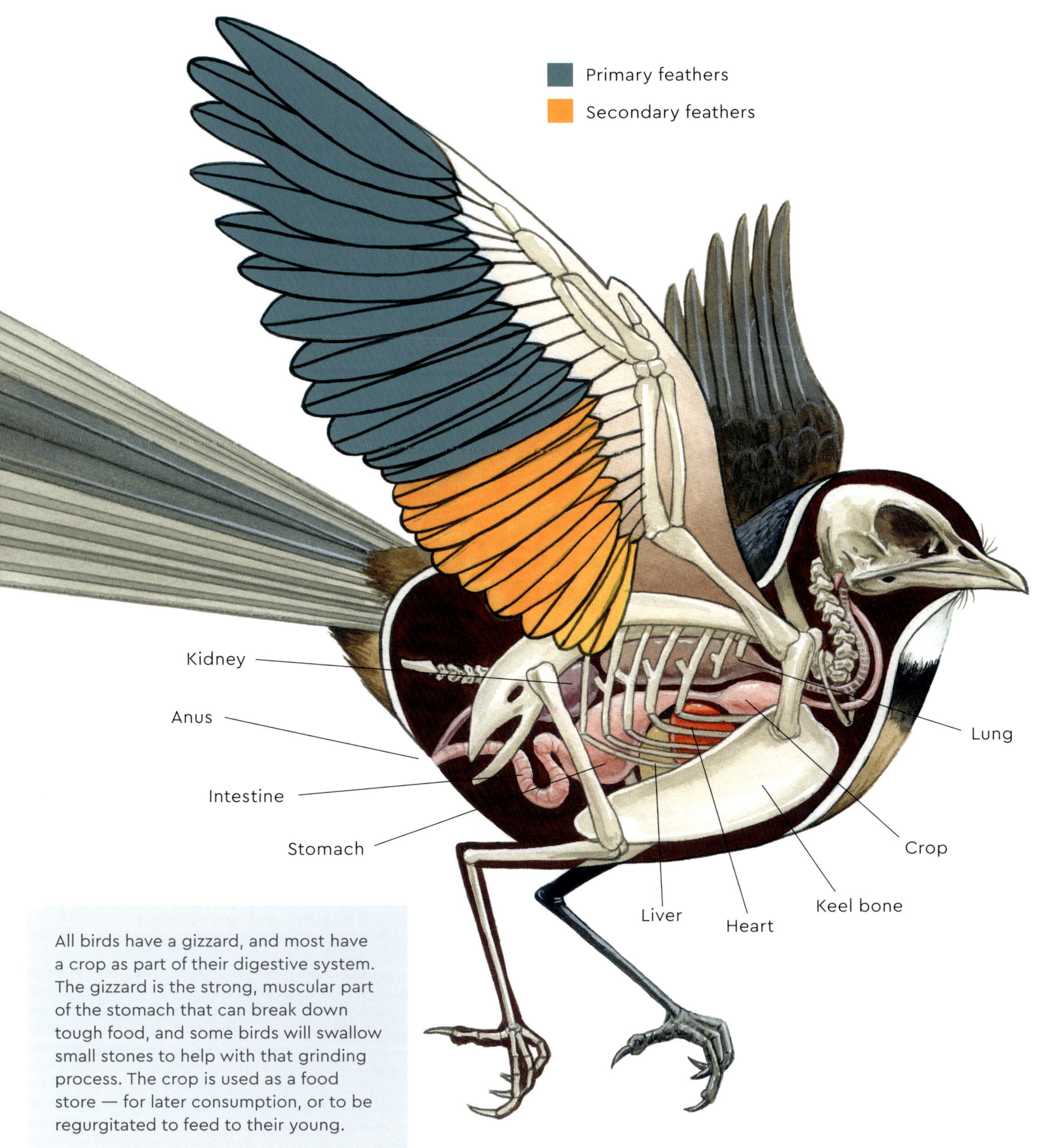

All birds have a gizzard, and most have a crop as part of their digestive system. The gizzard is the strong, muscular part of the stomach that can break down tough food, and some birds will swallow small stones to help with that grinding process. The crop is used as a food store — for later consumption, or to be regurgitated to feed to their young.

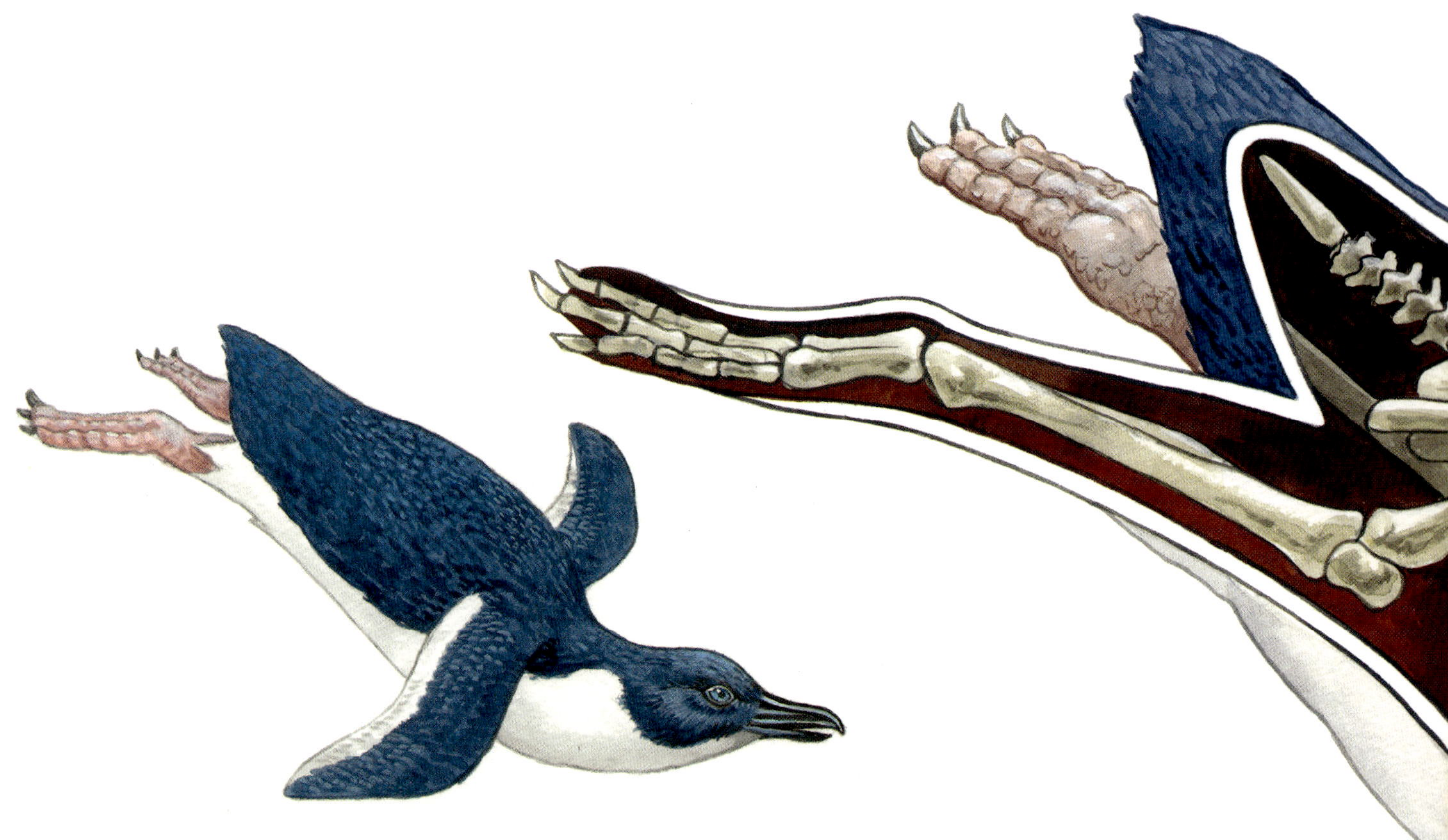

Little blue penguin | kororā

At just 40 centimetres in length, and weighing just over a kilogram, the little blue penguin is the smallest penguin in the world, and the most common species to be found around New Zealand's coasts — especially in the lower South Island and the upper North Island.

Penguins lost the ability to fly many millions of years ago, as they became diving birds, and their wings adapted more and more to swimming for prey, in preference to flying. The bones lost their slim, light nature and became much more dense and strong, and the wing shape gradually took on its more efficient 'flipper' shape, similar to that of other sea-hunters. Powered by robust muscles, the penguin is able to fly/swim through the water at speeds of around 3 to 4 kilometres an hour, although in a chase they can reach nearly 7 kilometres per hour — that's faster than a human's walking pace, and quite fast enough in the water for this little bird to catch fleeing fish. They prefer to hunt for small fish, squid and krill, and while they usually operate in water depths of about 2 to 20 metres, they can dive to 70 metres or more in search of prey. They can remain submerged for up to a minute before coming back to the surface.

Part of their scientific name — *Eudyptula* — means 'good little diver'.

It's quite common to see these penguins singly or in small groups in inner waters and harbours. They spend most of their days at sea and come ashore in the evenings. Nests are made under vegetation, in hollows and caves, and even under buildings near the shore — some birds will walk inland for up to a kilometre or more to find a spot that's to their liking, to nest and raise chicks.

Little blue penguins can live for about 6 to 10 years, although some can reach over 20 years in captivity.

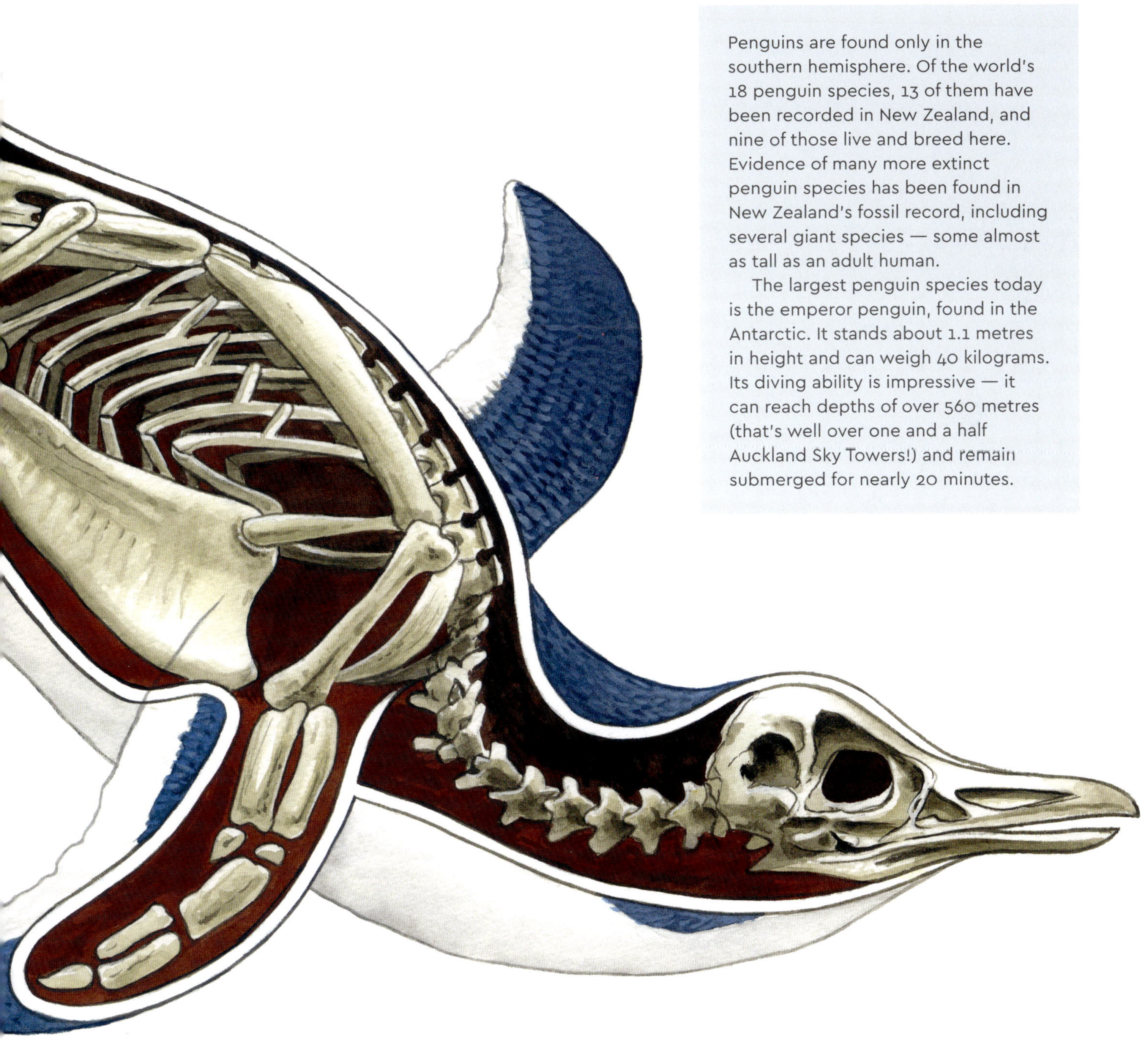

Penguins are found only in the southern hemisphere. Of the world's 18 penguin species, 13 of them have been recorded in New Zealand, and nine of those live and breed here. Evidence of many more extinct penguin species has been found in New Zealand's fossil record, including several giant species — some almost as tall as an adult human.

The largest penguin species today is the emperor penguin, found in the Antarctic. It stands about 1.1 metres in height and can weigh 40 kilograms. Its diving ability is impressive — it can reach depths of over 560 metres (that's well over one and a half Auckland Sky Towers!) and remain submerged for nearly 20 minutes.

Long-tailed bat | pekapeka

Bats are the only mammals to have developed true wings — using skin stretched between long 'fingers' — and proper, controlled flight. New Zealand has two main species: the long-tailed bat, and the short-tailed bat (I wonder how they came up with those names?).

The long-tailed bat is the smaller of the two species, and weighs about 8 to 11 grams; for comparison, the New Zealand $2 coin weighs 10 grams. Although numbers have declined, this bat is still widespread throughout much of the country, and it can sometimes be seen flying at dusk, when it awakes from its daytime roost from forest trees or from under natural or constructed dark overhangs — under bridges, for example.

They hunt prey while in flight — at speeds up to 60 kilometres per hour — taking any flying insects, such as beetles, flies, moths and midges — and often eating their own body weight in insects in a single night. Hunting in the dark, they can find and chase insects — and avoid obstacles — by means of echolocation.

The bat sends out low-frequency sound waves 10 to 20 times per second from its mouth or nose (sometimes these are audible to humans), and when they hit any object, the bat can 'hear' the echo in their large, sensitive ears. Their usual hunting range can be quite large — up 100 square kilometres.

Bats usually live for about 9–10 years.

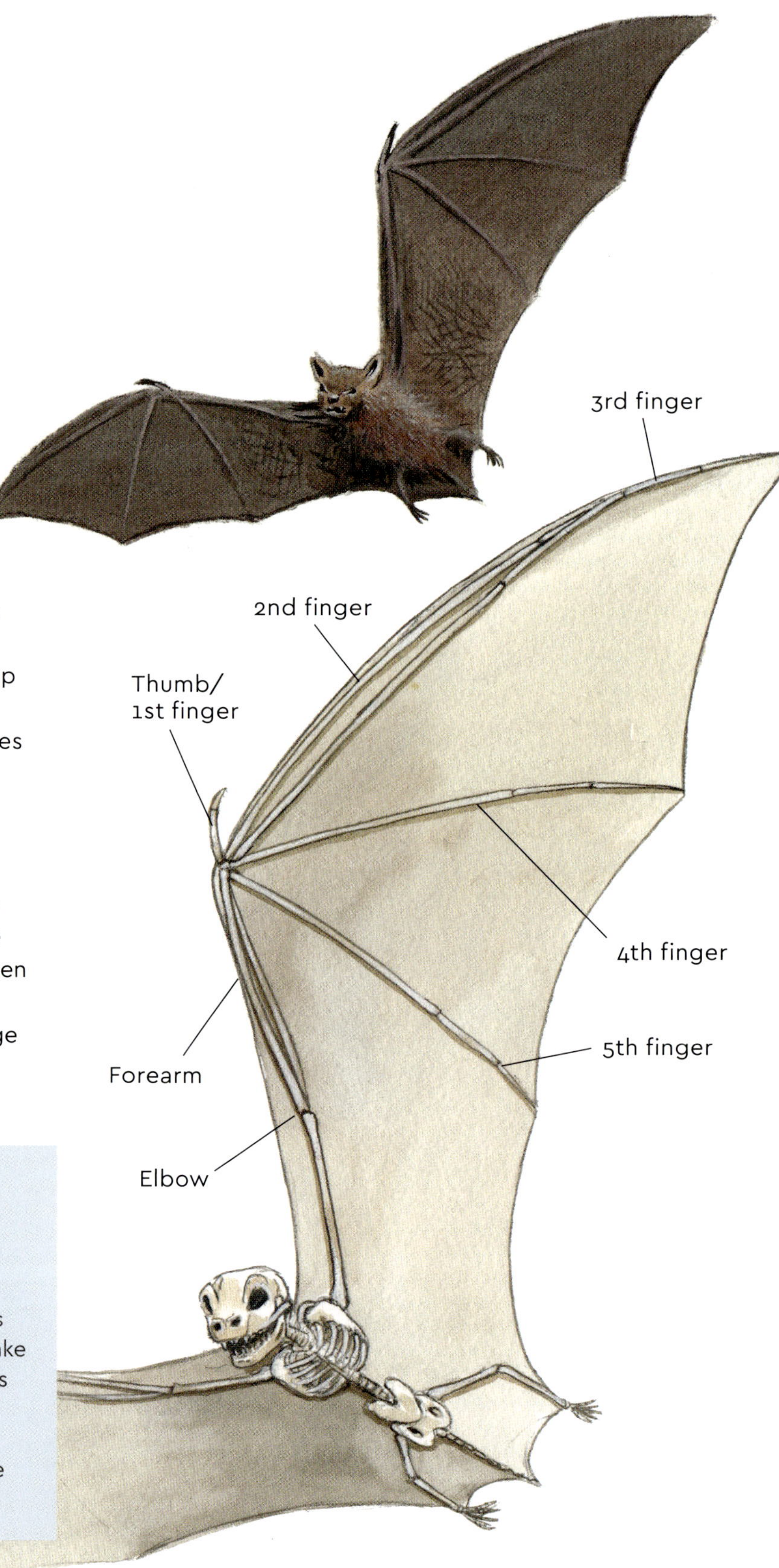

There are about 1100 different species of bat around the world, and they make up about 25 per cent of all mammals. Many are much larger and faster than New Zealand's bats — a species in Mexico has been recorded at speeds up to 160 kilometres per hour, which would make it the fastest mammal on earth. The largest bats are the 'flying foxes' of the Pacific region, with a wingspan sometimes reaching 2 metres. The smallest is from Thailand — the bumblebee bat is about the size of a human thumbnail!

Forearm homology

Nearly all animals need to move about in order to thrive — to seek food or prey, to find a mate, to rest or simply to explore. Creatures such as snakes and worms can get about by pushing and undulating their bodies, but the great majority of animals use limbs of one sort or another.

Insects, spiders and crabs and others are invertebrates, which means that they all have exoskeletons — their hard parts are on the outside. So their limbs are essentially hard tubes with muscles and nerves inside. Their legs — which vary in number — are of course used in locomotion (walking and running), with the front pair often employed as arms to catch prey, handle food, to clean themselves or to examine their surroundings.

'Higher' animals are called vertebrates, as their hard parts — their bony skeletons — are inside their bodies.

The general anatomies of invertebrates show distinct similarities, but the diagram below shows that it's even more pronounced in vertebrates, and it reveals clearly how evolution has changed and shaped animal life as different species evolved and adapted over many millions of years.

The bones of the arms (forward limbs) of most animals clearly show these strong similarities — called homology — even though they are all used for quite different purposes and are vastly different in size.

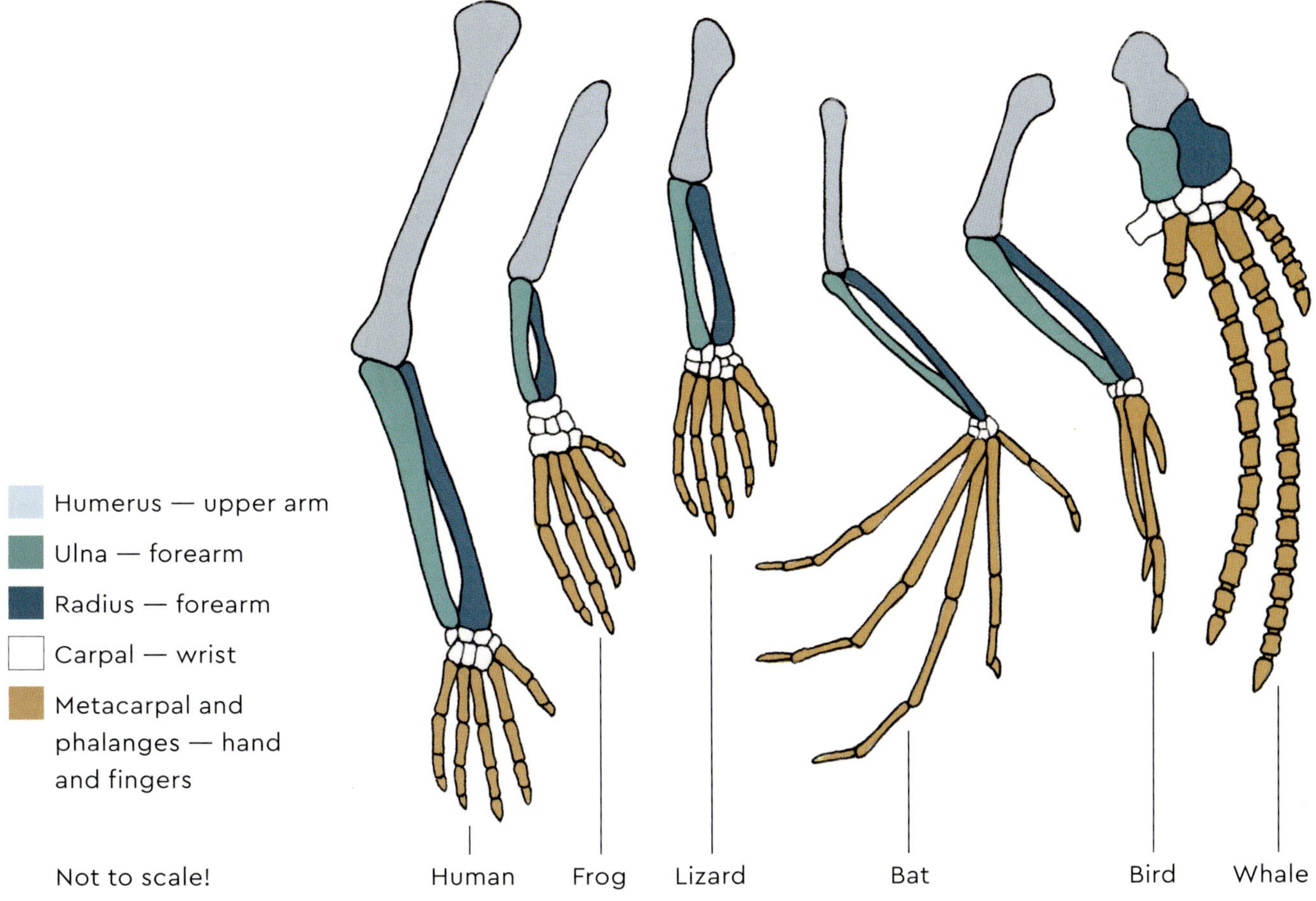

Fur seal | kekeno

There are about nine species of seals around New Zealand waters, and the most common is the New Zealand fur seal. These seals come ashore to breed at many locations around the South Island, and in the lower North island. At many other places they will haul themselves ashore in groups, or singly, simply to sleep or bask in the sunshine.

They feed mostly on small fish, octopus and squid, but will take conger eels and larger fish in deeper waters. They hunt for food mostly at night, when many deep-water fish species come closer to the surface.

The front flippers are used for swimming and also for getting about on land. Powerful muscles are attached to the substantial bones and shoulder blades of their fore-limbs, which enables them to achieve speeds of over 40 kilometres an hour when chasing prey — even at depths of 200 metres for over 10 minutes, or more . . . deeper and for longer than any other species of fur seal.

Under the skin of all marine mammals — seals, dolphins, whales and walruses — is a thick layer of protective oily fat, called blubber. The blubber is less dense than seawater, so it increases the seal's buoyancy, making it easier to float.

Besides being a form of insulation from the cold, the blubber is rich in protein and nutrients, so a seal isn't forced to continually hunt for food. It can spend time ashore to rest or to care for the young.

They have two layers of fur: a tough and long outer fur, with a softer 'woolly' fur underneath. The air trapped in this double layer waterproofs and insulates the seal, and together with the layer of blubber, the seal is well protected from the cold of the seas and the chill air when it's resting on land.

Males are larger than females and can reach up to 2.5 metres in length and weigh around 90 to 150 kilograms. They can live for about 15 years.

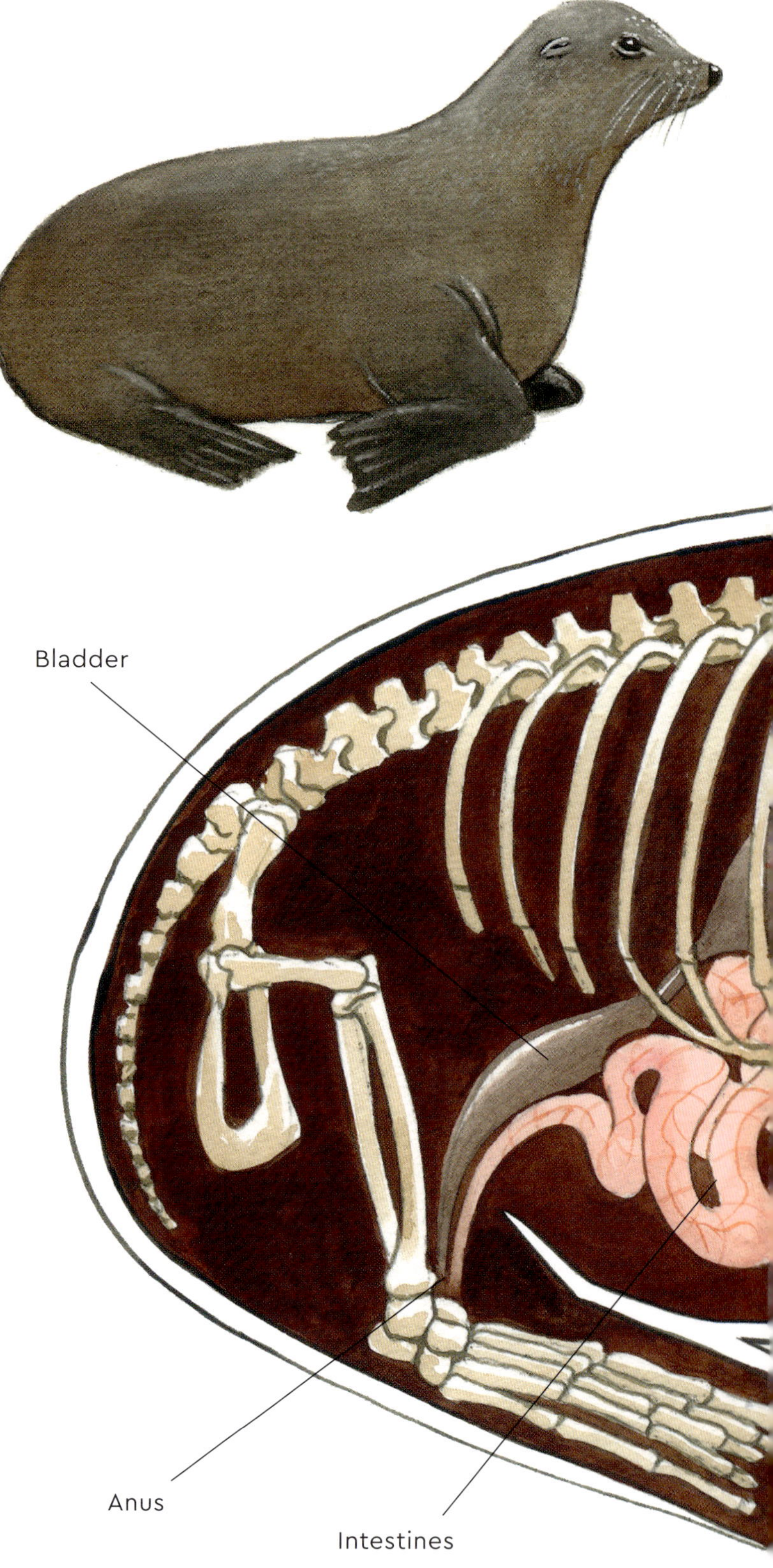

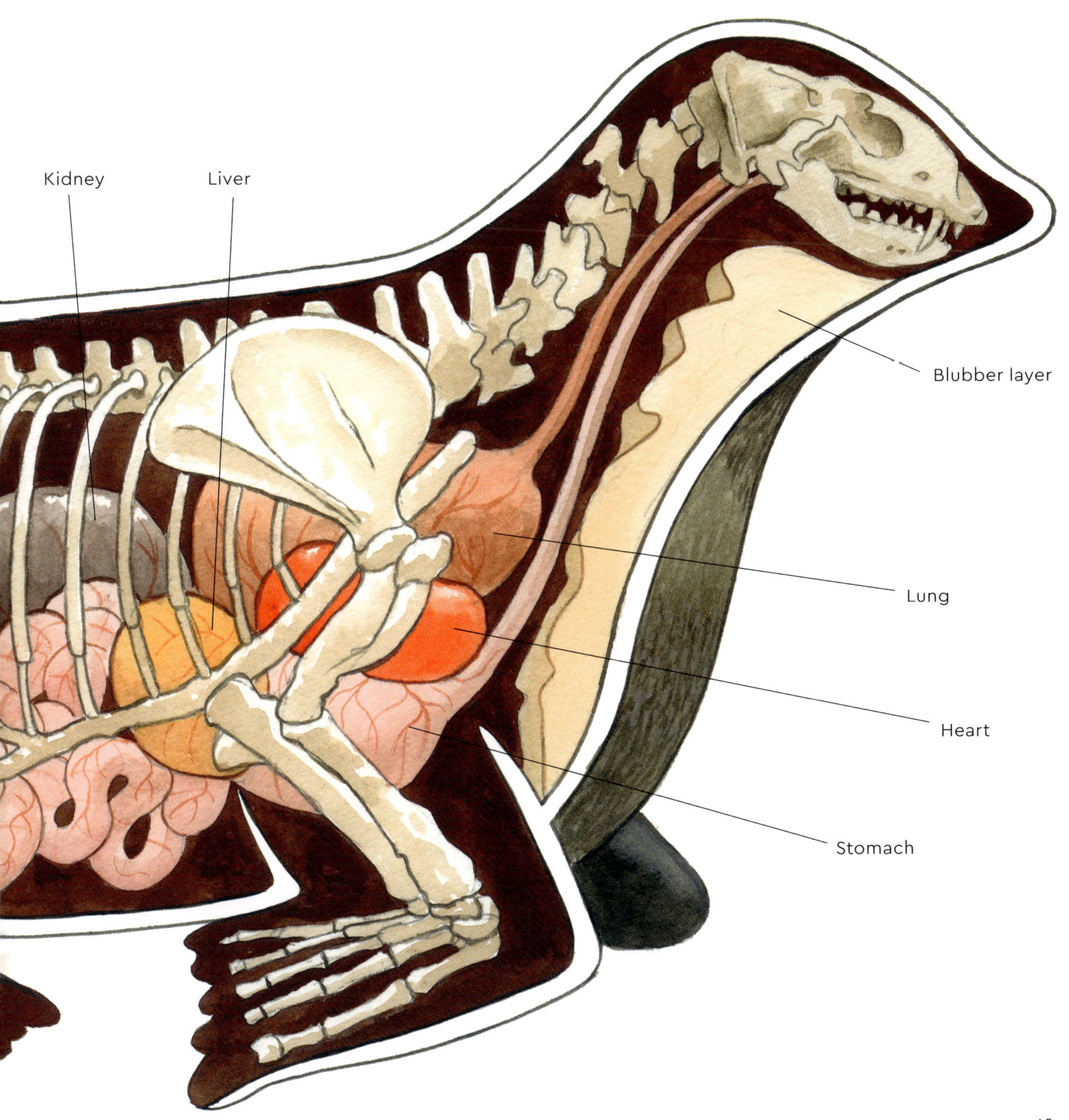
Kidney
Liver
Blubber layer
Lung
Heart
Stomach

Bottlenose dolphin | terehu

Dolphins are the smallest members of the sea-dwelling mammals called toothed whales. There are about nine dolphin species in New Zealand waters and more than 60 different species around the world.

The bottlenose dolphin is one of the most well-known and is quite common around our coastal waters. It's a large animal, and can reach up to 4 metres in length and weigh between 150 and 200 kilograms. They can live for up to 40 years.

Dolphins are very social animals, and usually travel in large groups, called pods, of anywhere between 10 to 25 (mostly females and young) individuals and up to 1000 or more (mostly males).

They can be found in all sorts of environments and feed on fish, squid, crabs and shrimps. They don't use their teeth to chew, but to grip — a fish is usually taken and then swallowed head first, so that fins and spines don't catch in the dolphin's throat.

Dolphins are very intelligent, and they will work as groups to 'herd' shoals of fish, play 'catch' with clumps of seaweed and interact with humans in the water.

Dolphins can't breathe 'automatically' while they sleep, as humans do. As they live in water, every breath they take needs to be controlled. They will rest and breathe at the surface of the water, 'half asleep' — the left side of the brain goes to sleep, while the right side controls breathing and remains alert, and the right eye closes. After a period of time they can switch about — the left eye closes and the brain's right side sleeps.

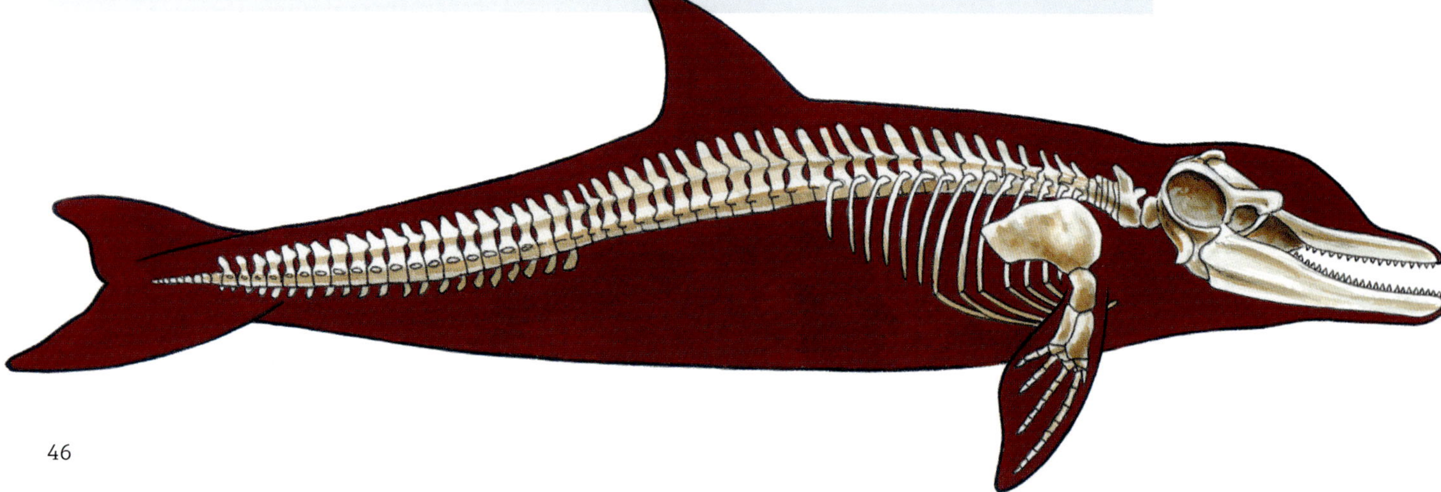

Dolphins and other toothed whales can find their prey by echolocation. They send sound signals out into the water which then bounce off any nearby object back to the dolphin. These sound waves actually travel five times faster in water than they do in air. The dolphin can understand and interpret the differences in the reflected signals to find prey, possible predators or other members of the pod.

The dolphins' sound signals can be quite complex and subtle. They use low-frequency sounds, like clicks and whistles, to communicate with each other and high-frequency sounds for echolocation.

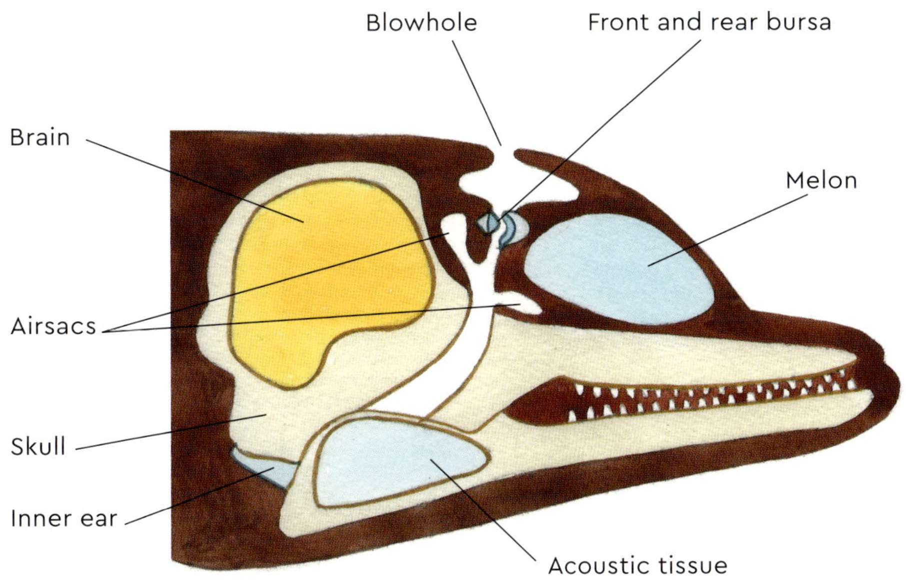

The sounds are created in the airsacs and 'shaped' into different frequencies by the melon (containing tissue and fluid, and acting as a sort of sound 'lens') and the phonic 'lips' near the dolphin's blowhole. Using structures call the front and rear bursa and the phonic lips, the bottlenose dolphin is capable of emitting clicks and whistles at the same time — quite an impossible feat for a human!

INDEX